The
Unfinished
War

The Unfinished War

Vietnam and the American Conscience

WALTER H. CAPPS

BEACON PRESS   BOSTON

Beacon Press books are published under the auspices
of the Unitarian Universalist Association,
25 Beacon Street, Boston, Massachusetts 02108
Published simultaneously in Canada by
Fitzhenry & Whiteside Limited, Toronto

Printed in the United States of America

(hardcover) 9 8 7 6 5 4 3 2 1

Library of Congress Cataloging in Publication Data

Capps, Walter H.
  The unfinished war.

  Bibliography: p.
  Includes index.
  1. United States – Civilization – 1970– 2. Vietnamese Conflict,
1961–1975 – Influence and results. 3. Vietnamese Conflict,
1961–1975 – United States. I. Title.
E169.12.C27 1982   973.92   81-66193
ISBN 0-8070-3260-3   AACR2

*For Shad Meshad and Bill Mahedy, whose
lives teach the meaning of the war*

Contents

The
Unfinished
War

1. The Unfinished War

"War is a strange sea, and once embarked upon, there is no foretelling where the voyage may lead."
— WINSTON CHURCHILL

THE HOSTILITIES ceased on May 1, 1975, but the Vietnam War isn't over. It is not yet over, and cannot be, for the 4.2 million American men and women who belonged to the nation's fighting force. It isn't over, and cannot be, for family and friends of the 57,692 men and women who died in the war, or for those still awaiting word of the 2,500 combatants identified as "missing in action." Such casualty figures are well known and have remained constant since 1975. Less known, and more immediately arresting, is the fact that since 1975 there have been as many suicides among Vietnam veterans as there were combat fatalities during the war itself. Equally compelling is the fact that the number of such suicides increases each year and, by Veterans Administration projections, is not expected to peak until 1990. By most estimates, there are a half-million Americans – both men and women – who carry the emotional and psychological wounds commonly referred to as "delayed stress reaction." Almost two and a half million veterans were exposed to Agent Orange. Approximately 30,000 are currently behind bars. Clearly, for them, the war is not over, nor for those who frequent the counseling centers of the Veterans Outreach Program across the country, nor for those who continue to plead for some sign of recognition, for some national homecoming celebration. The war is not only unfinished but beginning all over again for the children of the Vietnam War generation, who now seek to know just what happened to our nation in the turbulent 1960s and 1970s. Significantly, the reaction is much the same whether one experiences the war directly or views it as history through books, television, or reports from the participants.

The perplexity that occurs on Veterans Day, or over the Memorial Day weekend, when it becomes apparent that we cannot speak in a single voice or within one comprehensive framework of interpretation about the various wars in which the United States has been involved is a sign that the war is unfinished. The continuing controversy over the two low, sloping walls of black granite proposed as the national monument to honor Vietnam veterans in the nation's capital, on which the names of each American soldier killed in the war will be inscribed, is testimony to the same uncertainty. All of this indicates that the Vietnam War is not like World War I or World War II, which had clearly identifiable enemies, clearly identifiable causes, and comprehensible and convincing resolutions.

Until Vietnam, it may have been possible to say that war is war, a soldier is a soldier, and combat is combat. But the Vietnam War did not mean what other wars meant. It did not elicit the same American participation. Though the nation's leaders tried, they did not find an easy or satisfactory way to appeal to national zeal or patriotic responsibility. Americans felt and still feel differently about our involvement in Vietnam. Yet there is consensus on one point: The event was a national trauma, a rupture in the nation's collective consciousness, and a serious and somber challenge to the ways we wish to think about ourselves, our role in the world, and our place in human history.

On any day, the Vietnam War is given a prominent place on television, in newspaper headlines, and in the stories featured in national magazines. For instance, the "Calendar" section of the *Los Angeles Times* of September 16, 1981, carried an account of a new television film created by Stirling Silliphant, called "Fly Away Home," which ABC Television was scheduling for pilot presentation. Silliphant suggests in the article that the film embodies a unique concept. Recognizing that the Vietnam War was the "most divisive war for Americans since the Civil War," Silliphant decided to provide an overview, to present "every side of it, every position, including that of the Vietnamese, both North and South. No apologies," he contends, "no *mea culpa*, just an objective look at the war as if it had been fought one thousand years ago, as if I was writing a drama about the Trojan War." Then Silliphant criticizes other films that have appeared (*Deer Hunter, Apocalypse Now, Rumor of War*, and others) for being too slanted and not comprehensive enough. "I wanted to do a television *War and Peace* about Vietnam," he explains. "I wanted to present fully and completely a study of this war, which cost us 55,000 dead Americans and 450,000 casualties."[1]

In the "Metro" section of the same paper on the same day was news of the suicide of Clarence Stickler, a Vietnam veteran who had taken part in a hunger strike against the Veterans Administration the previous summer. He had been wounded by a grenade explosion in Vietnam and had protested that the Veterans Administration had ignored his plea for effective medical and psychological assistance. Stickler leaped to his death from the eleventh floor of a Los Angeles hotel, depressed, his friends related, because he was suffering from complications of delayed stress from his Marine combat service. His friends said that Stickler had been a good Marine in Vietnam, but had been troubled for years by his actions – killing Vietcong men, women, and children under orders. When he would reflect on this, a friend recalled, he would "cry like a baby."

On the day before Clarence Stickler's funeral, some of his associates in an organization of Vietnam veterans gathered outside the VA hospital in Wadsworth, California, and accused the Veterans Administration of criminal negligence in connection with the suicide. A spokesman for the group, William Rigole, secretary of the Veterans Coalition, referred to Stickler as "a soldier who died because the VA was unresponsive and irresponsible." The same group of veterans was planning a candlelight vigil for Clarence Stickler in front of the hospital on the coming Sunday.[2]

People magazine the same week featured a story about David Christian, who at age eighteen had been the youngest second lieutenant ever to graduate from the Army's Officers' Candidate School. During an eight-month tour in Vietnam,

Christian had collected two Congressional Medal of Honor
nominations, seven Purple Hearts, two Bronze Stars, two Silver
Stars, a Distinguished Service Cross, two Vietnamese Crosses
of Gallantry, and a chestful of additional medals. Then, dis-
abled by napalm burns in 1968, David Christian had left the
military (at twenty-one years of age) and become the Army's
youngest retired captain. His fighting spirit was not quieted
when circumstances forced him to leave the battlefield, however. Returning home to find a public weary of the war and
often hostile toward participants, Christian launched a campaign for veterans' rights. Along the way he founded a group
called the United Viet Nam Organization, in which he serves as
executive director.

The article quotes David Christian as saying, "Now we're
looking forward with great expectations to see what Reagan
will do. We're hoping, we're praying, and we're about to raise
hell. I want the Vietnam issues answered – Agent Orange, the
delayed stress syndrome, psychological readjustment." Then he
asks, "Why the high unemployment rate and high suicide rate
and high incidence of marital problems among Vietnam vets?
Why all the 'why' if the Vietnam vets have been fairly treated?"[3]
Christian believes that the country treats its welfare recipients
and prisoners better than it treats the veterans of the Vietnam
War.

David Christian could depend upon the support of Lynda
Van Devanter, who was an army nurse in the central highlands
of South Vietnam during the war. In the spring of 1979, Van
Devanter found herself screaming, then crawling combat-style
across her living room when the siren of a police car sounded in
her Long Island neighborhood. The wailing noise was the same
kind that signaled rocket and mortar attacks in Vietnam. Her
crawling was a scrambling for safety. She had been back from
Vietnam for eight years before such flashbacks occurred; it had
taken that long for the trauma to break through. Not until the
siren sounded did she perceive connections between her war
experiences and her heavy drinking, continual crying, inability
to hold a job, and incapacity to form a close relationship with a

man. Since the day of recognition in 1979, Lynda Van Devanter
has been working with women veterans of the war who suffer
from delayed stress.

Among the 7,465 women who served in Vietnam is Cissy
Shellabarger, a Texas nurse, who continues to dream about
tending wounded soldiers being brought to her on stretchers. In
her dreams, when Shellabarger bends down to pick up a shoe,
she finds a foot inside. It is a dream she has had repeatedly.

The war is unfinished for David Christian and William
Rigole. It isn't over for Lynda Van Devanter or Cissy Shellabarger either. It wasn't yet over for Clarence Stickler.

It isn't finished for Henry Kissinger, United States secretary of state under Presidents Nixon and Ford, who on September 16, 1981, went to Grand Rapids, Michigan, to help celebrate
the opening of the Gerald Ford Presidential Museum. Responding to a newsman's questions on a wide range of currently
important national and international topics, Kissinger referred
to the Vietnam War as "a terrible tragedy into which the United
States should never have gotten involved." He added that the
ordeal put the world into a "prolonged nightmare of over eight
years."

Clearly the war goes on for William Westmoreland too,
commander-in-chief of U.S. and allied forces in Vietnam from
1963 until the cessation of hostilities in 1975. For on another
day, November 19, 1981, General Westmoreland was quoted in
the press as saying that the liberal protestors at home had been
largely responsible for whatever lack of military and political
success the United States suffered in Vietnam. As the former
leader was speaking, a conference began in New York City to
analyze the Vietnam War through the perspective of some six
years' distance. Throughout the conference, antagonisms
among American interpreters—who continued to find themselves contending against each other, just as they had during
the war—threatened to disrupt the proceedings. Back again
were Daniel Ellsberg, of Pentagon Papers fame; Gloria Emerson, author of *Winners and Losers*; William P. Bundy, a key figure in the State Department during the war; Barry Zorthian,

who headed the U.S. Public Affairs Office in Saigon during the war and who monitored (some say sanitized) much of the news transmitted back to the homeland, and still others who played key roles. *The Washington Post* headline for its news story covering the conference read "At Vietnam Reunion, Not-So-Friendly Fire."[4]

Clearly, Vietnam remains unresolved in people's minds, even for those who played crucial roles in both its execution and its interpretation. The divisions and differences of opinion dramatically evident during those years have continued during the period of retrospective evaluation. Indeed, it sometimes seems as if the intervening years have done little beyond polarizing the attitudes, pro and con, prevalent during the war. All of this might have been expected, given the nature of the trauma and the depths it reached in the American soul.

Certainly the issue has not been laid to rest in Baileyville, Maine, a papermill town with some two thousand inhabitants whose school board voted unanimously in April 1981 to remove Ronald Glasser's book, *365 Days*, from the high-school library. The authorities objected to Glasser's use of harsh language in a series of vignettes of soldiers critically wounded in battle in Vietnam. Glasser's defense was that "only four-letter words would capture the anguish of the soldiers he depicted." The issue received national attention because a student in the local high school challenged the ban, filing a class action suit against the school committee for its alleged violation of students' First Amendment rights. The challenge was supported by the state's Civil Liberties Union. The case is expected to be heard eventually by the U.S. District Court in Bangor, but before those deliberations take place the citizens of Baileyville once again have become involved in emotional discussions about the meaning of the war in Vietnam.

On Christmas Day, 1981, four veterans of the war returned to the United States after visiting Hanoi in the country of their former enemy. They had gone, the veterans said, to learn more about U.S. soldiers still listed as missing in action and to acquire more accurate information about the effects of Agent

Orange, the chemical defoliant which during the war years had been widely spread over Vietnamese jungles. Representing Vietnam Veterans of America, Robert Muller, executive director and former Marine, expressed gratification about the journey's achievements. "We accomplished more than we intended," Muller said at a press conference in New York's Kennedy International Airport. "We started a genuine dialogue, not as politicians but as former soldiers." A second member of the group, Michael Harbert, a former Air Force sergeant, agreed, saying, "We went in peace, and we met in peace, and I think for me and for all of us the war is really over."[5]

Yet on December 28 (the day the Christian liturgical calendar commemorates the "slaughter of the innocents"), other veterans of the war denounced the Hanoi visit. Some charged that the four had been used by Hanoi to secure reparations from the United States for damages inflicted upon the country. Al Santoli, a veteran, a reporter for the *National Veterans Review*, and the editor of a book, *Everything We Had* (a collection of portrayals of the war by combat participants), was particularly critical of the group for placing a wreath at the tomb of Ho Chi Minh. "You are a total disgrace to every one of us who served in Vietnam," Santoli told Muller and the others.[6]

This sharp difference of opinion was perhaps to be expected. In 1979, during an interview on a public television information program, Arthur Schlesinger, Jr., said that the American people were just beginning to receive the first preliminary drafts of attempts to place the meaning of the war in an intelligent framework. Schlesinger conjectured that it would take at least another five years for the definitive account to develop. While expositions of a war are sometimes offered immediately after hostilities cease, a longer period is required to place the experience into appropriate perspectives of descriptions and analyses, and particularly when the subject is as full, complicated, and interlaced with puzzles and irresolution as the Vietnam War is. Some have suggested that the process will take much longer, citing the fact that World War I had perhaps not been seen clearly until Paul Fussell issued his

excellent book *The Great War and Modern Memory*, which first
appeared in 1975. The larger truth may be that understanding a
war is an ongoing process, never fully accomplished.

When I mentioned to a friend, a professor of theology in
Germany, that I had been turning more and more of my attention to the subject of the Vietnam War and America's reactions,
he commented with still-vivid memories of postwar Germany
that it seemed curious to him that so little had been written by
Americans, particularly on the religious aspects of and
responses to the Vietnam experience. He had expected Americans to go through a process of self-evaluation, self-criticism,
and self-judgment – something of the collective "dark night of
the soul" – similar to that which Germany had experienced
following the Nazi era. He wondered where there was evidence of this. Perhaps, he continued, the collective conscience
of America had suffered so much during the war years, we
found it necessary to find some respite after the hostilities had
ceased before we could undertake any thorough examination
of implications.

Yet the very opposite is plausible too; virtually everything
that has happened in the United States since the end of the
Vietnam War can be seen as both reaction and response to the
war. Perhaps the responses have not been as overt as in Europe
following the defeat of Nazi Germany, probably because the
catalyst was not as specific and the outcome not as decisive, but
they nevertheless are there.

The several national opinion surveys that have been conducted in recent years confirm America's continuing preoccupation with the war. The Connecticut Mutual Life *Report on
American Values in the '80s: The Impact of Belief* found religious
commitment to be the factor that most consistently and dramatically affects American values and behavior.[7] To attribute
the current prominence of religion to Vietnam War aftershock
is too easy, but the connection is certainly implicit. Religious
belief seems to revitalize American self-confidence, and this
may have occurred in the wake of those events in the 1960s and

1970s that symbolize the disillusionment that Americans now wish to overcome. The survey that was the basis for George Gallup and David Poling's *The Search for America's Faith* produced correlative findings. Seeking to understand the significant growth of conservative religion within the nation, Gallup and Poling point to a concerted effort to revitalize cherished American institutions such as the family and the church following an era when these became disarrayed. When people describe the disarray, they mention the Vietnam War as a prominent causal factor.[8]

Certainly the recent rise of Protestant conservatism, sometimes referred to as the New Right or the new religious right, bears direct connection with individual and corporate wrestling over the ramifications of the Vietnam experience. The belief and actions of Dr. Jerry Falwell, of Thomas Road Baptist Church, of the "Old Time Gospel Hour," and of the Moral Majority blend a re-enunciation of conservative or fundamentalist religious themes with a strong appeal to patriotism, frequently expressed in highly militaristic terminology. Indeed, the context within which Falwell is calling Christians to show allegiance to the Gospel is one in which the forces of good and evil are competing against each other from diametrically opposite positions. When these forces are then identified with the "free world" and its adversary, and further as America and Russia, or the American way of life and the Communist way, it is evident that the issue behind the Vietnam War continues. In this view, the Vietnam War stands as one event in a series through which an age-long conflict is being enacted. Furthermore, the reemergence of conservative tendencies, as expressed in Falwell's style of religion, can be seen as evidence of a profound discontent with the outcome of the war in Vietnam as well as a desire to make certain that the next skirmish "comes out right." Thus, one can argue responsibly that the rise of the Moral Majority has direct linkages with the impact of the Vietnam War. Joseph McCarthy sounded similar conservative notes less than five years after the cessation of hostilities of

World War II in 1945. A similar conservative reaction prevailed in American life following the Civil War.

The revitalization of conservative religion is not the only discernible development in American social and cultural life which can be traced to the war experience. The new spirituality, too – the rise of contemplative religion, the daily practice of meditation by significant segments of the citizenry, and even the new and perceptibly strong interest in mysticism – is also related. This side of the American conscience (or soul) has emerged powerfully and eloquently since 1975 and coincides with preoccupation with personal needs during a time when an agreed-upon, collective sense of meaning is difficult to identify or attain. Christopher Lasch has brilliantly documented this tendency in *The Culture of Narcissism*, the theme of which is echoed by such other writers as Morris Dickstein and Richard Sennett. Books on the new individualism in our society are matched by such recent magazines as *Self*, dedicated to the discovery and promotion of "self-power." In each issue *Self* offers articles on how to develop successful strategies to promote one's well-being – "how to know what you want, and get it!" The *Los Angeles Times* offers the equivalent through an insert, *You*, which became a regular weekly feature in 1981. Such cultural emphases are mirrored by the growing number of people who are exploring the more individualistic and individualizing elements within world religious traditions. We have cited the dramatic turn to mysticism; in the same category is the return of prayer groups and impressively well attended Bible study groups. Retreat centers are full to overflowing throughout the country. Even monasteries – once thought to be out-of-the-way places intended primarily for a small number of religiously endowed individuals who prefer relative seclusion – are now being frequented by people seriously interested in what monks have to teach and what the monastic life offers as a way of living and ordering one's life. While all of these activities depend upon group interaction, in various degrees, they support the tendency to emphasize the power of religion primarily in personal and individual rather than in social and political terms.

All of the indicators of a powerful recovery of the contemplative and spiritual strands within religion are appropriate responses that surface when collective confidence wanes. No clever sleight of interpretive hand is needed to trace these developments to the impact of the unfinished war in Vietnam.

But this is just the beginning. It is intriguing to try to place these developments together, to view each in the light of the other. T. George Harris does precisely this in his introduction to Jeffrey K. Hadden and Charles E. Swann's book *Prime-Time Preachers: The Rising Power of Televangelism*. Following leads provided by David Riesman in *The Lonely Crowd* and *Individualism Reconsidered*, Harris approaches the rise of conservative religion in individual and privatistic terms. He mentions the insights of Christopher Lasch, along with Tom Wolfe's famous essay "The Me Decade." But Harris gives the same references a significant twist. It is all too true, he recognizes, that "Americans are losing faith in corporations, government, schools, churches, medicine, political parties, the press, marriage, parenthood" – the traditional institutions. But while doing so, Americans are coming to expect much more of themselves. They are striving toward self-fulfillment and demonstrated achievement, almost exclusively through individual resourcefulness.

> In marriage, for instance, a woman now expects herself to be an accomplished bedmate, an intellectual equal, a wise and loving mother, perhaps a fellow jogger and tennis partner and smart tourist, one who continues to grow, a community organizer and cohost, often a co-professional, and almost always a fellow breadwinner. We expect similar miracles from ourselves at work; aside from earning the highest pay ever known, we expect to be sensitive to co-workers, enlarge our education, make a social contribution, and do very little damage to the environment.

Harris recognizes both individualism and selfishness in such tendencies. However, he believes individualism pertains

most directly to placing dependence upon oneself in lieu of on
the institutions of the society, as one might have expected in
previous generations. This turnabout has led to a new model of
personality, the lonely striver, who is marked by a willingness
to stretch his or her talent to the limit.

> It's no accident that jogging has become a national
> obsession . . . or that the drive for health and physical
> well-being stays at the top of the rising-demand list
> identified year after year in our monitors of changing
> values. Nor is it strange, in a nation turned inward to
> demand heroic effort from the self rather than out-
> ward toward reliance on institutions, that today's
> mystical surge should focus upon the possible interior
> powers of the God-given body/mind and especially
> upon healing.

Concluding, Harris suggests that "as life comes to feel more and
more like that supreme test of self, the marathon run, our
national behavior moves further into the 'privatization' trend."
How does this relate to the rise of conservative religion?
The answer is in the means through which conservative religion is chiefly transmitted – that is, in television.

> Television becomes the inevitable tool for the lonely
> striver's worship. Just as media campaigns have taken
> over from the political party, so the prime-time
> preachers in their powder-blue suits and cocky smiles
> have stepped proudly up to deliver the church's
> sermons. They are smart and tough. Ever more
> sophisticated in their use of the computer as well as of
> television – the paired technology that raises millions
> by its combination of exciting programs and direct
> mail – the preachers have now gained an earthy new
> sense of power through their Reagan victory.[9]

In short, the individual resourcefulness of the lonely
striver is encouraged and nourished by the pastoral work of the
television evangelists. In this sense at least, the individualistic
trends that Lasch and others have documented seem to
correlate with the recent rise of conservatism. And both, in
ways we shall specify in the following chapters, directly relate
to ways in which the experience of the war is being assimilated
and accommodated.

These are significant components in assessing the impact on America of the war in Vietnam. To treat such factors properly, we must reconstruct the political, religious, and intellectual background against which the reaction is taking place. Wars never occur in isolation, as if military events on soil beyond our borders prompted a variety of social, political, cultural, religious, and individual emotional responses at home. On the contrary, the Vietnam War was fought in many places, on many fields, on many planes, all at the same time. The formal military activity was restricted to Indochina, but as Lawrence Lichty and Peter Braestrup have reminded us, the war was also fought on television. Furthermore, it was waged on college and university campuses. One recalls the uprisings in Berkeley, the National Guard at Kent State, and the burning of the Bank of America building in Santa Barbara. On every campus, in every city square, and in virtually every living room a complex and multidimensional battle took place.

The conflict was enacted in less obvious ways, too – not only in direct conflict, argumentation, protest marches, sit-ins, and rallies, but in changes in styles of art, music, and literature, and in shifts in modes of dress and manners. One could tell on which side of the issues people stood by the clothes they wore, the vocabulary they used, the literature they cited, the music they listened to, and of course the length and style they wore their hair.

Some said that the fundamental quarrel was not about the potential threat of communism in Vietnam, but about what it is to be an American, and indeed, what the future course of humankind ought to be.

As the events both at home and abroad, overt and subjective, worked their way, it became apparent that two contrasting American cultures had come into being. The differences in the ways each looked and thought became sharper than ethnic, racial, or economic distinctions. Two kinds of value systems had been spawned, with fissures deeper than those between Protestants and Catholics. Families were split, less by natural generational differences than by divergent attitudes, sensitivities, temperaments, and fundamental allegiances. The Biblical prophecy that when the great day comes, brothers will be turned against brothers, fathers against children, and children against parents seemed to have been fulfilled in the existing tensions. Each side complained that the other didn't understand what was happening. The other side responded that it couldn't understand because it couldn't hear.

Fundamentally, the Vietnam War was a contest between two views of human priorities. Because those ways became so sharply divided, the question became whether the American story could ever again be told as a single narrative account or whether the nation's involvement in the war in Vietnam made such cohesiveness impossible.

This, then, is the question that has haunted all Americans since the formal cessation of hostilities. Can there be a continuous account of American history, or does Vietnam symbolize a break in the narrative sequence?

Morris Dickstein writes in *Gates of Eden* that the Vietnam experience meant much more than military defeat:

> In Vietnam we lost not only a war and a subcontinent; we also lost our pervasive confidence that American arms and American aims were linked somehow to justice and morality, not merely to the quest for power. America was defeated militarily, but the "idea" of America, the cherished myth of America, received an even more shattering blow.[10]

Dickstein believes that "Vietnam made us sick, made us feel like exiles," and, most of all, it "robbed us of an image of this nation that we desperately needed." He added, "By marching we tried to purge ourselves of the least trace of inner complicity with the war; we stepped outside the national consensus and reached out for solidarity with others who shared an alternative idea of America."[11] Because of the terms in which the conflict was waged, in Dickstein's view, the outcome is to be seen primarily in changes of "sensibility, awareness, and attitude, not of institutions." And those interpreters of the war who do not share Dickstein's point of reference would nevertheless tend to agree with his conclusions—namely, that what was being debated were conflicting or alternative *ideas of America.*

Neither side could accept the other's fundamental concept. Those who protested the war objected from the first to the idea that America was being locked into a battle to the end with Communist-inspired international forces. Those who perceived world events in terms of this basic ideological conflict believed that their opponents had become "soft on communism" and subversive of the nation's cherished interests. Thus it was the idea of America that was tested and contested.

The outcome was a hung jury. Neither side could claim victory or was satisfied, yet neither would acknowledge defeat. Indeed, neither was quite sure what the outcome was. Thus, no one could find much to celebrate when the hostilities ended.

Further, no one knew quite how to receive the nation's warriors when they returned from battle. There was no welcome, no banners, no festive ceremonies, no parades down the main streets of the cities and towns to the cadence of John Philip Sousa's triumphant marches. When the idea of America was placed in jeopardy, so were all the other precepts and practices that depended upon the principal one for sustenance.

What could it mean to be a hero when everybody recognized we had lost? How could patriotism be defined in a situation in which obedience to military orders in some people's opinion meant further destruction of American values? What could it mean to be a warrior when there were profound questions concerning the identification of the enemy? How could the conflict even be called a war when it never exhibited any clear strategy to support deliberate progress toward the achievement of clear military objectives?

These are only some of the reasons that there were sharp differences of opinion as to the real battleground. The Vietnam War forced elements of the supposedly healthy American conscience to take sides against each other. It placed the rudiments of the American sense of identity at odds with each other. Thus Americans' responses following the cessation of military hostilities have been an attempt to resolve conflicts, to achieve restitution, and to follow the strange pathway of collective self-consciousness to conclusion.

The intentions of this book would not be served if we built cases that laid the blame at the feet of certain factions, institutions, politicians, military strategists, the national leadership, protestors, or even flaws in the American character. The intent is to do more than reiterate the oft-repeated judgment that the war was a colossal mistake in which the United States should never have become implicated. Merely to repeat the antiwar and/or prowar rhetoric of the rallies of the 1960s and early 1970s won't assist our purposes either, for by now those speeches belong to the body of materials one must analyze, not to the interpretive categories providing exhaustive explanation.

Yet it is essential to take as a premise that the war was a tragedy, a dramatic event with an ending that was inevitably unhappy because integral elements eluded successful resolution or closure. To qualify as tragedy, an event must allow us to probe human nature fundamentally, with total seriousness, and the war in Vietnam did this most visibly. Viewing it as tragedy, we can identify ways in which we are accommodating the trauma—if indeed we are—in contemporary American self-consciousness. We want to learn more about how we are assimilating it into our self-understanding. These objectives lead us to the subject of American religion.

As we shall see in the following pages, a veritable outpouring of potent self-criticism, prolonged frustration, and renewed enthusiasm has appeared in the sentiments and judgments on the unfinished war. There are compelling reasons to believe that the most pronounced social trends in the post-Vietnam era are based on images of America that Americans most wish to retain. There is also evidence that the restoration of a compelling idea of America can only follow the healing of the American conscience. This raises questions as to how the collective conscience shall be ordered, and what it will require its guardians to do before the healing and the restoration can occur.

From every side, competing ideas about the nature of America are under scrutiny. From every side, America is being perceived as a post-Vietnam America. There is as yet no consensus that the idea of America that we must develop is the same as the idea we had before. This is eloquent testimony to the power of the trauma we call Vietnam.

2. Certain Inalienable Rights

"Please, don't worry. I pledge my word that Ho Chi Minh will never sell his country."

— HO CHI MINH

WE ARE FAMILIAR with much of the background, yet it seems that in certain senses the war always was and will continue to be. Its origins lie not in any single event or act of provocation, but in intrinsic tensions in the principles that harbor and support colonial rule and in the dramatic and necessary change of the world during the first decades of the nuclear age. Add the dramatic movement of American society from infancy to an elicited maturity in which the nation came increasingly to assume major responsibility for the structure and order of the world, and the formal hostilities in Vietnam became a stage on which a large number of not always related plots were acted out: the "free world's" fear of communism; the United States' alliances with the countries of Western Europe, particularly France, following World War II; the profound changes occurring within the Asian world (particularly in China); the new power acquired in the postwar years by the Soviet Union; and of course a civil war in Vietnam.

Given the coincidence of these dimensions, the real question is, *why in Vietnam?* How did it happen that all of these plots were acted out on Asian soil? How did they become entangled and intermeshed with the divergent interests of warring local factions within an exceedingly small country? And why was the United States enticed to exercise its newly acquired maturity in an environment whose rules of conduct it hardly knew? By what means was it persuaded to allow its successes and failures in local skirmishes to reflect its performance in other challenges? Why did it choose to make Vietnam the crucial testing ground, drawing the line there and declaring "this far, and no further"?

Some of the scenes apparently fit, but the central plot seems to have been transplanted from somewhere else. The actors too were primarily "imported," and many of the issues became attached to Vietnamese soil by the projection and attribution of outsiders.

This made the Vietnam conflict symbolic, even mythological, from the outset. The ideological battles eventually became more real and substantial than anything taking place on the field, which placed the combatants in grave danger, for they were not trained for mythological warfare. Besides, there was no real consensus as to how to read the symbolism. The driving conflict was over alternative interpretations of mythological events. When the skirmishes ended, the larger, sweeping, pervasive, and mythological contest continued to be fought in ever more serious terms.

We cannot retell the story from the first, but as Arthur Schlesinger, Jr., said, part of what it is to come to terms with Vietnam is to identify the incentives and motivations that led to America's involvement. We thus feel the obligation to sketch in some of the components of the complicated drama.

In about 1000 B.C., the tribe of Giao-chi, inhabitants of the southern portion of China, made its way into what is now Vietnam and through cross-breeding and transmutation became the people subsequently called the Vietnamese. In the third century B.C. more Chinese came, taking over the country by force. The area was named An Nam, the "pacified south" – that is, the area south of China. Chinese influences became formative. The sociocultural temper of the area was characterized by a blending of Buddhist religion, Confucian ethics, and mandarin government, civil service, and education.

For more than a thousand years the indigenous Vietnamese were governed by Chinese overlords, though there were numerous rebellions. Not until A.D. 939 was Chinese rule effectively overthrown, yet Vietnam continued to be riddled with internal strife, which made it vulnerable to repeated Chinese invasions. In the fifteenth century, the warrior Le Loi

broke the hold of the Chinese once again, proclaimed himself
emperor of Vietnam, and established the Le Dynasty, which
was to last for three centuries. But even during this period the
country was divided by struggles between strong mandarins in
the north and those in the south. These internal divisions were
exploited by the colonial powers—notably the French, Dutch,
Portuguese, and British—who by the sixteenth and seventeenth
centuries were looking to the area for possible commercial gain.

Religious interests were involved at this time too, for
French colonial activities were carried out in cooperation with
the missionary efforts of the Catholic Church. As early as the
sixteenth century the Dominicans established a missionary
base near the city of Faifo (known later as Da Nang), from
which they set out to bring Christian teachings to the people in
surrounding Indochina and China. By the early seventeenth
century, the Jesuits, expelled from Japan, were allowed to enter
Vietnam. Within a short time French, Spanish, Portuguese, and
Italian missionaries were active in the country, with the French
eventually gaining the greatest power and influence. In 1664
the French East India Company and the Society of Foreign
Missions were established to work cooperatively. Their power
and influence came only within the midst of intense and continuing internal strife as well as in competition with the other
outside forces interested in the territory.

By the middle of the eighteenth century France had
become the dominant colonial power in Vietnam. But the
efforts of the French missionaries were not welcomed by those
who governed Vietnam, who perceived Christian teaching as a
direct threat to their own authority. By the end of the eighteenth century many French missionaries had been persecuted
and forced to leave the area. During the reign of Ming Mang
(1820–1841), for example, a number of French missionaries
were killed and their Vietnamese followers were executed.
Thus, after 1840 French missionaries sought the direct assistance of French troops in carrying out the next stages of coloni-
zation. Between 1841 and 1847 the squabbling heightened into
intense fighting. Many missionaries were expelled and some

were sentenced to death, though none was actually executed. In the aftermath, Parisian authorities decided that direct military intervention was needed.

The French conquest of Vietnam was initiated in 1858, under Napoleon III. Vietnamese resistance was stiff. France captured Saigon in 1859 but was unable to take the countryside. For two years the French were able to maintain only a small garrison in Saigon, but in 1861, with fresh reinforcements, they captured the surrounding territory. In 1862 the mandarin administrators of Vietnam signed a peace treaty with the French, giving them title to Saigon and the three southern provinces. Four years later, Vietnamese resistance weakened further, and French rule was extended over the whole of Cochinchina, the name the French used for the provinces of South Vietnam. Thus the distinction between the northern and southern parts of Vietnam was sealed. The French called the north Tongking and the south Annam; the natives called the north Bac Bo, the center Trung Bo, and the south Nam Bo.

France continued its attempt to take the entire country and even to extend its rule into the territory of Cambodia until 1873, when it decided to put new emphasis upon strengthening its position within Europe. Correspondingly, it could give less emphasis to the ambitions of colonial conquest. But by 1882 it had recovered sufficient strength at home to reinitiate its efforts toward colonial expansion. After sending various military expeditions into the north and bombarding North Vietnamese coastal cities from the sea (principally from the Gulf of Tonkin), France was able to impose its will by force. On August 25, 1883, the mandarins signed a treaty that made both Annam and Tongking protectorates of France. In 1893 France annexed Laos too, then both Thailand and Cambodia, and formed the Indochinese Union.

French colonial rule over Vietnam continued from 1883 until 1939, when Japanese occupation of the country began with the outbreak of World War II. During this long period the French established various forms of industry to capitalize on Vietnamese raw materials: rice, coal, rubber, and rare minerals. With the imposition of certain modern methods of farming, crop production increased, to the benefit of French colonial power far more than of the Vietnamese people.

It is the familiar story. Such conditions breed resentment, which inspires rebellion, which makes the dream of eventual self-rule attractive. Vietnamese uprisings against the French were the rule of the day. But not until the beginning of the twentieth century did interest in nationalism become concerted enough for the Vietnamese to plan their rebellions carefully.

In 1905 and 1906, under the influence of Phan Boi Chau, a thinker and writer, and the new emperor, Cuong De, an organization called the Association for the Modernization of Vietnam came into existence. Chau and Cuong De actively courted the assistance of the Japanese, whose primary help was to provide education for hundreds of bright Vietnamese who were smuggled to Japan to study.

In 1907 Chau opened his own school, the Free School of Tongking, in Hanoi, and it quickly became the center and source of strong anti-French sentiment. In 1908, under its influence, mass demonstrations against heavy taxation occurred. The French reacted by arresting the demonstrators and sending some into concentration camps on the island of Poulo Condore, in the South China Sea. France also called upon Japan to stop its support of Vietnamese resistance, which it did after it received a loan from France in 1910. Chau and Cuong De were expelled from Japan and fled into China, where in 1912 they set up a government in exile, with Cuong De as president. Chau was imprisoned in China for a time, and his movement realized no significant growth during the First World War. After the war, in 1925, he was kidnapped by French agents, returned to Vietnam, and condemned to death; the verdict was altered to enable him to live in confinement in his house in Hue, where he died in 1940. Though modest in intent and lacking dramatic accomplishment, Chau's movement did indeed encourage anticolonial discontent, and belongs to the succession of developments leading eventually to emancipation.

The same years witnessed continuing though scattered and fundamentally unintegrated efforts toward achieving nation-hood, including uprisings, rebellions, and growing intellectual dissatisfaction with French rule. Various nationalist organizations came into being, the most important and influential of which was the Vietnamese Nationalist Party, founded in 1925 under the leadership of Nguyen Thai Hoc – who changed his name in 1943 to Ho Chi Minh.

If ever there was a candidate for psychohistorical interpretation, it was Ho Chi Minh, whose adopted name is virtually synonymous with the cause he represented. Ho was the central figure in the revolutionary drama in which the entire Vietnamese population eventually came to be involved. He stood as the symbol of the Vietnamese desire for liberation from the oppression and inequities of French rule, and it was through his diplomatic leadership and political savvy that that liberation was attempted, and by some accounts achieved.

Ho was born on May 19, 1890, and died on September 3, 1969. Throughout his life he had the reputation of a person who sought adventure. He loved to travel and was curious about the world beyond the borders of his homeland.

In 1911 he left Vietnam aboard a merchant steamer, the *Admiral Latouch Treville,* working his way as a cabin boy, steward, and sailor. In 1913 he lived briefly in London, working as a snow shoveler and stoker and eventually as a kitchen assistant in the Carlton Hotel in order to learn English. While in London, Ho became fascinated with the Irish struggle for home rule; he also joined an organization called Lao Dong Hai Ngoiai (Workers Overseas), consisting of Asians living in London who wished to combat colonialism.

When World War I began Ho was in France, but his fear of being called up for military service encouraged him to go to sea again. The ship on which he worked sailed in 1915 to the United States, where Ho came in contact with the Ku Klux Klan, the plight of black Americans, and protest strikes against American involvement in the war. By the end of the war Ho was back in France, where in 1920 he joined the Communist Party. In the next years he traveled to the Soviet Union and to various parts of China, striving all the while to keep in close touch with developments within his own country.

By this time Ho's vision had been formed by a constellation of convictions. He was opposed to imperialism in all forms. He was intrigued by the teachings of Marx and Lenin and was schooling himself in the processes by which communism had developed in other countries; he was fascinated by the variety of indigenous structures and emphases it could assume, depending upon the social circumstances and the general conditions of life in those places where it seemed most appropriate. He searched for the form that best fit Vietnamese life and culture, and when he had devised it, he wished to supplant the succession of foreigners by which his native land had been ruled for centuries.

Such convictions became explicit in 1920 during the Socialist Congress at Tours. Recognized as the Indochinese delegate, Ho was asked his opinion as to how the Communist promise of a world revolution might be accelerated. He responded:

> Today, instead of contributing together with you to world revolution as I should wish, I come here with deep sadness and profound grief, as a Socialist, to protest against the abhorrent crimes committed in my native land.
>
> You all know that French capitalism entered Indochina half a century ago. It conquered our country at bayonet point and in the name of capitalism. Since then we have not only been oppressed and exploited shamelessly, but also tortured and poisoned pitilessly. (I would stress this fact that we have been poisoned, with opium, alcohol, etc.) I cannot, in but a few minutes, reveal all the atrocities perpetrated by the predatory capitalists in Indochina. Prisons outnumber schools and are always overcrowded with detainees. Any native suspected of having socialist ideas is arrested and sometimes put to death without trial. So goes justice in Indochina for in that country there is one law for the Vietnamese and another for the Eu-

ropeans or those holding European citizenship. The former do not enjoy the same safeguards as the latter. We have neither freedom of the press, freedom of speech, freedom of assembly, nor freedom of association. We have no right to emigrate or travel abroad as tourists. We live in utter ignorance because we have no right to study. In Indochina the colonialists do all they can to poison us with opium and besot us with alcohol. Thousands of Vietnamese have been led to a slow death and thousands of others massacred to protect interests that are not theirs.

Comrades, such is the treatment inflicted upon more than twenty million Vietnamese, that is more than half the population of France. And yet they are said to be under French protection. The Socialist Party must act effectively in favor of the oppressed natives.[1]

In the next years Ho worked out his philosophical principles and programmatic intentions. He wrote regularly for various Communist-oriented periodicals, commented frequently on events that had some relationship to the struggles in his own country, and seized every opportunity to call attention to colonial exploitation. He also denounced the effects of the work of the church, saying to the Fifth Congress of the Communist International in 1924:

Besides this wolfish administration [the French conquest], one should mention the Church. The Catholic Mission alone occupied one quarter of the areas under cultivation in Cochinchina. To lay hands on those lands it used unimaginable methods: bribery, fraud and coercion . . . Availing itself of crop failures it gave the peasants loans, with their rice-fields as security. The interest rates being too high, the peasants were unable to pay off their debts and their mortgaged fields went to the Mission. Using all kinds of underhand methods, the Church succeeded in laying hands on secret documents that could harm the authorities, and used these to blackmail them into granting it all it wanted. It entered into partnership with big financiers for the exploitation of the plantations granted free to them and the lands stolen from the peasants. Its henchmen held high positions in the colonial government. It fleeced its flock no less ruthlessly than the

planters did. Another of its tricks was to get poor people to reclaim waste land with promises that it would
be allotted to them. But as soon as the crops were
about to be harvested, the Mission claimed ownership
of the land and drove out those who had toiled to
make it productive. Robbed by their "protectors" (religious or lay), our peasants were not even left in peace
to work on their remaining tiny plots of land. The land
registry service falsified the results of the cadastral
survey so as to make the peasants pay more taxes.
These were made heavier every year. Recently, after
handing over thousands of hectares of land belonging
to Vietnamese highlanders to speculators, the authorities sent bombers to fly over these regions so that the
victims dared not even think of rebelling.[2]

Ho told the congress that the natives in the French colonies
were "ripe for insurrection" but lacked leadership and organi-
zational skill, and he called upon the Communist International
to "help them to reorganize, supply them with leading cadres,
and show them the road to revolution and liberation."[3]

In 1925, under Ho's influence, the Revolutionary League of
the Youth of Vietnam was founded. This served as nucleus for
the work of the Communist Party in Vietnam (the Indochinese
Communist Party), which was officially established in 1930.
Appealing for assistance during the founding of the party, Ho
described the post–World War I situation in Vietnam:

[The] war resulted in untold loss of life and property
for the peoples. French imperialism was the hardest
hit. Therefore, in order to restore the forces of capitalism in France, the French imperialists have resorted
to every perfidious scheme to intensify capitalist
exploitation in Indochina. They have built new facto-
ries to exploit the workers by paying them starvation
wages. They have plundered the peasants' land to
establish plantations and drive them to destitution.
They have levied new heavy taxes. They have forced
our people to buy government bonds. In short, they
have driven our people to utter misery. They have
increased their military forces, first, to strangle the
Vietnamese revolution; second, to prepare for a new
imperialist war in the Pacific aimed at conquering

new colonies; third, to suppress the Chinese revolution; and fourth, to attack the Soviet Union because
she helps the oppressed nations and the exploited
working class to wage revolution.[4]

Looking ahead, Ho envisioned that

World War II will break out. When it does the French
imperialists will certainly drive our people to an even
more horrible slaughter. If we let them prepare for
this war, oppose the Chinese revolution and attack the
Soviet Union, if we allow them to stifle the Vietnamese revolution, this is tantamount to letting them
wipe our race off the surface of the earth and drown
our nation in the Pacific.[5]

He pleaded that instead of working separately, the Vietnamese
might join together, working through the Indochinese Communist Party "to lead the revolutionary struggle of our entire
people" for independence, democratic freedom, self-rule, education for all, an equitable distribution of financial resources,
and full "equality between man and woman."[6]

None of these transformations would have happened had
there not been a growing awareness of the suppressive characteristics of colonialism. At the same time, none of it could
effectively take place beyond the watchful and wary eyes of
the French rulers.

Predictably, revolts, clashes, open rebellion against the
French, and increasing dissatisfaction and uneasiness moved
Vietnam more and more toward open confrontation. Known to
be the leader of the rebel cause even though he influenced it
from beyond the Vietnamese borders, Ho was arrested in Hong
Kong in 1931 by the British. He spent much of his imprison-
ment in the hospital receiving treatment for tuberculosis.
When he was released in 1933, Ho fled to Moscow, and in 1934,
while recuperating from the aftereffects of the disease, he
enrolled in the International Lenin School and began a period
of relative quiet, with time for study and reflection.

However, this situation changed dramatically when the
Japanese invaded China in 1937. In 1938 Ho was back in China
familiarizing himself with the teachings of Mao Zedong and

traveling from north to south, east to west. In 1940, after World War II had begun in Europe and the Japanese had occupied Vietnam, Ho secretly crossed the border into his native land. Together with some Vietnamese revolutionaries who had fled from the French, he took refuge in caves along the Chinese border. He renamed the mountain adjacent to this jungle hideout at Pac Bo "Karl Marx" and the nearby river "Lenin."

Here Ho and his comrades conceived of the political organization which would eventually drive the French from Vietnam. Here, in exile, on May 19, 1941, they founded the Vietnam League for Independence, a movement better known as the Vietminh. Here, in exile, Ho Chi Minh issued the now-famous "Letter from Abroad" in which he declared that the time for decisive action had come:

> Elders! Patriots! Prominent Personalities! Intellec-
> tuals! Peasants! Workers! Traders and soldiers! Dear
> fellow-countrymen!
> Since France was defeated by Germany, its power
> has completely collapsed. Nevertheless, with regard
> to our people, the French rulers have become even
> more ruthless in carrying out their policy of exploi-
> tation, repression and massacre. They bleed us white
> and carry out a barbarous policy of all-out terrorism
> and massacre. In the foreign field, bowing their heads
> and bending their knees, they resign themselves to
> ceding part of our land to Siam and shamelessly sur-
> rendering our country to Japan. As a result our people
> are writhing under a double yoke of oppression. They
> serve not only as beasts of burden to the French
> bandits but also as slaves to the Japanese robbers.
> Alas! What sin have our people committed to be
> doomed to such a wretched fate? Plunged into such
> tragic suffering, are we to await death with folded
> arms?
> No! Certainly not! The twenty-odd million descen-
> dants of the Lac and the Hong are resolved not to let
> themselves be kept in servitude. For nearly eighty
> years under the French pirates' iron heels we have
> unceasingly and selflessly struggled for national inde-
> pendence and freedom . . . If we were not successful,
> it was not because the French bandits were strong,

but only because the situation was not ripe and our people throughout the country were not yet of one mind.

Ho continued:

> Now, the opportunity has come for our liberation. France itself is unable to help the French colonialists rule over our country. As for the Japanese, on the one hand, bogged down in China, on the other, hampered by the British and American forces, they certainly cannot use all their strength against us. If our entire people are solidly united we can certainly get the better of the best-trained armies of the French and the Japanese.

Then comes the direct call to action:

> Fellow-countrymen! Rise up! Let us emulate the dauntless spirit of the Chinese people! Rise up without delay! Let us organize the Association for National Salvation to fight the French and the Japanese!
> The hour has struck! Raise aloft the banner of insurrection and lead the people throughout the country to overthrow the Japanese and the French. The sacred call of the Fatherland is resounding in our ears; the ardent blood of our heroic predecessors is seething in our hearts! The fighting spirit of the people is mounting before our eyes. Let us unite and unify our action to overthrow the Japanese and the French.[7]

Conditions were certainly ripe for change when the Japanese occupation began in 1939. Eighty percent of the population remained illiterate; only 15 percent of the children had received any education at all. Only one university had been established for the twenty million inhabitants of the country, primarily for use by the French. Fifty percent of the people owned no land at all, and virtually half of the territory was owned by less than 3 percent of the landowners.

But Ho had to wait until 1945 for the realization of this dream. From 1939 until the end of the war the people of Vietnam lived under Japanese occupation. All accounts confirm that the Japanese permitted the resident French colonial authorities to continue exercising power over the people, but the Japanese possessed the real control, which discredited the French even more in Vietnamese eyes. This political condition, combined with the increasing hardships that were imposed upon the people, created a climate in which the desire for revolt and emancipation from oppression became omnipresent. As the French grew weaker and weaker, the Vietminh was able to give both leadership and specific purpose to the growing hostility.

Nevertheless, the people were operating at cross purposes. Revolutionary movements with objectives similar to those of the Vietminh were competing for the allegiance of the citizenry, and Ho's most immediate fear was that the revolutionary movement would become so dispersed as to encourage social and political fragmentation. He found it necessary to discourage, even suppress, rival parties and forces for change when these competed with Vietminh ambitions.

Nineteen forty-five was unquestionably the most important year in the revolutionary struggle of the Vietnamese people. By this time Ho had amassed an army of some five thousand men, whom he had been training in the north during the occupation. In March 1945, out of some desperation with the situation both in Vietnam and more comprehensively in World War II, the Japanese deposed the puppet French government. In the same month the Vietminh, working closely with an American intelligence unit, waged an intensive and effective guerrilla war against their new colonial masters.

The American presence in Vietnam was prompted by a desire to defeat the Japanese wherever their power was evident, and thus the United States and the Vietminh were allies. Of course, this relationship was to be affected by the Japanese surrender in August 1945. Immediately following that event the Vietminh stepped into positions of local power, since no one else possessed the same strong residential authority. The Japanese had deposed the French; now they had been removed by a combination of local insurgents and United States military power. It was therefore appropriate to regard the de facto rulers as legitimate, though they were always under the watchful eyes of the Americans – the real conquerors.

On September 2, 1945, the Vietnamese people gathered to celebrate the Allied victory. United States war planes circled the city of Hanoi; on the reviewing stand, American army officers stood alongside Vietminh military leaders. The Vietnamese band played "The Star-Spangled Banner," and General Vo Nguyen Giap spoke glowingly of his country's "particularly intimate relationship with the United States."

When it was Ho's turn to speak, he began by quoting from the Declaration of Independence:

> "All men are created equal. They are endowed by their Creator with certain unalienable Rights; among these are Life, Liberty, and the pursuit of Happiness."
>
> This immortal statement appeared in the Declaration of Independence of the United States of America in 1776. In a broader sense, it means: All the peoples on the earth are equal from birth, all the peoples have a right to live and to be happy and free.[8]

After illustrating that the same convictions are fundamental to the Declaration of the Rights of Man, enunciated at the time of the French Revolution in 1791 – "All men are born free and with equal rights, and must always remain free and have equal rights" – Ho proceeded to describe the situation that made a Vietnamese declaration of independence possible:

> When the Japanese surrendered to the Allies, our entire people rose to gain power and founded the Democratic Republic of Vietnam.
>
> The truth is that we have wrested our independence from the Japanese, not from the French.
>
> The French have fled, the Japanese have capitulated, Emperor Bao Dai has abdicated. Our people have broken the chains which have fettered them for nearly a century and have won independence for Vietnam. At the same time they have overthrown the centuries-old monarchic regime and established a democratic republican regime.[9]

Clearly Ho did not intend simply to demonstrate the colleagueship he felt with the United States. More pointedly, he was taking advantage of the opportunity to link his revolutionary movement with the classical American revolutionary movement. After all, both peoples had had to fight off the oppression and inequities of colonial rule, had sought emancipation from the dictatorial powers of authority imposed from outside, had perceived inequalities between the entitlements of the overlords and those of the ruled, and had searched for alternatives to a state of life in which nationalism was thwarted by the people's status as possessions. And both had sensed that the tides of historical, social, and political change would deal benevolently with their desires for emancipation and self-rule. From virtually every vantage point, Ho believed, the Vietnamese revolution was supported by the same spirit that had brought about American independence in 1776.

In their weakened condition, the French could offer no strong resistance, yet the situation that prevailed on September 2, 1945, was not to continue without significant alteration. As soon as they felt able, the French moved to regain their empire in Indochina. It was far easier for them to regroup in the south than in the north, for they had always been stronger there, and Ho's forces had a more tenacious hold in the north. In very little time the French took virtual control of the southern portions of the country, set up headquarters in Saigon, and reestablished Bao Dai as emperor; they encountered very little direct or forceful resistance.

Postwar French incentives were straightforward and easily comprehensible. Ravaged by the brutal struggle with the Germans, France needed to rebuild. The clearest way to do this was to try to reestablish itself as a world power. Thus, immediately after the surrender of the Japanese and the Vietnamese declaration of independence, the French sought to come to new terms with those in command in the north, the Vietminh. Discussions between the two sides were initiated in 1945 and continued through 1946.

The Vietminh were understandably suspicious. They had had their fill of colonial rule. The French offered the Vietnamese dominion status, rather than the former colonial status, and full French citizenship. The Vietminh insisted on self-government and independence, and also sought unification of the southern and northern portions of the country, since the south was rich in the agricultural resources necessary to support the north, where the bulk of the population was concentrated.

On May 31, 1946, Ho traveled to Paris for negotiations regarding a French-Vietminh alliance, but he reassured his countrymen:

> Please, don't worry. I pledge my word that Ho Chi Minh will never sell his country.
> You in Nam Bo have been fighting self-sacrificingly for many months now to safeguard the territorial integrity of Vietnam; for this, our entire people are grateful to you.
> You in Nam Bo are citizens of Vietnam. Rivers may dry up, mountains may erode; but this truth can never change.[10]

The interests of the two parties were simply not compatible. What the French called dominion status was recognized by the Vietnamese nationalists as a revised form of colonial rule. He told his colleagues:

> As we desire peace we have made concessions. But the more concessions we make, the more the French colonialists press on, for they are bent on reconquering our country.

He reassured them that he would not accede.

> No, we would rather sacrifice all than lose our country. Never shall we be enslaved.
> Men and women, old and young, regardless of religious creed, political affiliation and nationality, all Vietnamese must stand up to fight the French colonialists and save the Fatherland.[11]

Under the impulse of their recent successes, the Vietnamese held out for nationalism, independence, self-rule, and the right to manage their own affairs through self-designated and nationally sensitive democratic processes.

Tensions mounted. Suspicions increased. Hostilities became greater and more frequent. Violence erupted. In

November 1946 the French shelled the harbor in Haiphong, killing more than six thousand Vietnamese citizens. On December 19 the French attacked Hanoi, and on December 21 Ho Chi Minh appealed to the French and the world for his country's independence, citing the pending preliminary agreements on a negotiated settlement.

But the war was already under way. It was to last almost thirty years, that is, until 1975, when U.S. President Gerald R. Ford welcomed home the last of the American troops. Somehow the United States had become aligned against Ho Chi Minh, in support of and in place of the French and in defense of colonial rule. The symbolism of the United States' presence and potential influence in Vietnam was ambivalent from the first.

3. Friends Become Enemies

"When the tough get going, the going gets tough."
— Peter De Vries

IT IS IMPORTANT to emphasize that the terms of the United States' entry into Vietnam were vastly different from those of France's. For one thing, Vietnam had never been an American colony. The United States had no reason to regard the Vietnamese as either a potential enemy or a client state. President Franklin D. Roosevelt expressed more than once his opposition to the policies France had been exercising in Vietnam; he preferred to place all of Indochina under an international trusteeship to prepare its people for eventual independence.

But such an attitude was not appreciated by the British who, while not a colonial presence in Indochina, nevertheless were interested in maintaining colonial arrangements. Thus, at the famous Yalta discussions in February 1945 Roosevelt felt obliged to alter his stand. He went on record as favoring that the colonies be placed in international trusteeship only with the approval of the "mother country." Obviously, France was unwilling to grant such approval, so there was no firm basis on which international trusteeship could become a reality for Vietnam.

Roosevelt died in April 1945, and Harry Truman became the new President. Truman was not greatly worried about the renewed colonial aspirations of either the British or the French. Instead, his attention was directed to what was called "the growing Soviet menace." The division of land among the four Allied powers after the war had made the Soviet Union the strongest nation in Europe and Asia. Virtually all of Eastern Europe was already under its rule, and even by 1945 the United States and its Western allies suspected Joseph Stalin of having broad global designs. The U.S. reaction was to erect bulwarks in Western Europe to keep Soviet expansion in check.

This also became the primary incentive to American policy regarding the French in their hostile relationship with the Vietnamese. President Truman wished to strengthen the Western alliance to be able to withstand any Soviet threat. Clearly this entailed rebuilding the power of France. Truman thus modified Roosevelt's stand on Vietnam, withdrawing U.S. support of international trusteeships and providing assurance to France that the United States would not be party to any attempt to take colonial territory away from former colonial powers. In the course of discussions with French President Charles de Gaulle, Truman extended a personal reassurance that the United States would not interfere with France's efforts to restore its sovereignty in Indochina. Yet it was evident that France was not powerful enough on its own to achieve this goal, so the United States asked France to recognize Vietnamese nationalism and to modify the terms through which it would exercise extended dominion status.

Fully cognizant of what was happening, Ho Chi Minh appealed to the United States in 1947 for assistance, arguing that Vietnam might be "a fertile field for American capital and enterprise." Such a request illustrates the flexibility implicit in Ho's understanding of Communist identity: Vietnamese communism was to be as indigenous and pliable as the Buddhist religion had been for centuries. It was also to be opportunistic, even to the point of taking advantage of capitalist incentives if they would give it strength. As part of his appeal, Ho even suggested that the United States might establish a naval base in Camranh Bay.

The U.S. response deserves careful scrutiny, for it gives a clear indication of the attitude of official America at this juncture to the situation in Vietnam and Indochina and to the Communist threat. United States diplomatic and intelligence agencies checked carefully to determine whether Ho was in league with the Soviet Union. At this time they found no such evidence; indeed, they clearly understood Ho to be a Vietnamese nationalist first, to whom the Communist form of government was an appropriate mechanism for throwing off oppressive colonial rule. A U.S. State Department report prepared at the time put it simply: Ho should be regarded as "the symbol of nationalism and the struggle for freedom to the overwhelming majority of the population."[1]

But in the postwar years it was becoming more and more difficult to appreciate the subtleties of such distinctions. Americans were becoming more and more alarmed about the possibility that the Soviet Union was working to take over the world. It was not Communist ideology per se that they feared, but the potential strength of the only other national power able to challenge the United States for world supremacy. Communism threatened the American way of life because it guided the actions of the nation that was perceived to be most menacing, the Soviet Union, which was after all transmitting patriotic literature that served notice of a future Communist dominion, and daring to say that its own form of government would one day prevail.

Thus it became exceedingly difficult for Americans to view Ho Chi Minh, with his avowed Communist leaning and his Marxist allegiances, as someone other than a ruler who might facilitate Soviet ambition in Indochina. In the popular imagination, communism was communism. Because the Soviet example was uppermost in mind, communism came to stand in sharp contrast to the democratic and capitalistic way of life that prevailed within the "free world." The possibility that Ho Chi Minh might be or become a puppet for the Russians, as the French rulers had been puppets for the Japanese, seemed eminently real. Wasn't it to be expected that when the chips were down Ho would side with the Russians or Chinese—the people of Asia—rather than with the Americans, who seemed to support Vietnam's former colonial masters?

Eventually, it was George C. Marshall, secretary of state in the Truman administration, who put into words what many within the government had been thinking: The United States was "unwilling to see colonial empires and administrations supplanted by philosophies and political organizations emanating from the Kremlin."[2] Thus, in time Ho Chi Minh came to

be included, accurately or not, within that network of leadership that constituted the greatest threat to the United States. To
aid the Vietnamese nationalists, directly or indirectly, was to
provide our adversary with assistance and thus to function at
cross purposes. Secretary Marshall said it forcefully and un-
ambiguously: The United States would not take any step or
provide any incentive that might assist a Communist triumph
in Indochina.

The evolution of U.S. policy is clear. In the beginning, the
United States wished to resist becoming either anti-Ho or pro-
France if this meant selecting an exclusive option. During the
Truman years it still wanted to have the best of both situations.
Certainly America was not opposed to Vietnamese nationalism,
nor could it wholeheartedly favor French colonial rule. But in
the course of postwar realignments its primary concern was the
evident expansionist tendencies of the Soviet Union.

Recognizing this to be the fundamental issue, the government wished to steer a middle course. While not granting Ho's
requests for aid, it also rejected French requests for military
assistance – an action that probably carried very little actual
force except in terms of propaganda, for what the French did
not receive in direct response to a specific request they did
receive through the U.S. Marshall Plan. Established to rebuild
Europe and restore those countries that had been blighted by
the war, the plan provided the French with sufficient resources
to develop their own weaponry and reestablish effective military might.

From the time of the bombing of Haiphong Harbor in 1946
until well into 1950, the fighting between the French and the
Vietnamese nationalists intensified. As the war progressed, a
number of related events influenced U.S. policy toward Ho and
the anticolonial forces. In 1949 Chiang Kai-shek's government
in China collapsed. The Communists gained control under the
leadership of Mao Zedong, and indications were that Mao and
his army were moving southward. Fears arose in the United
States that coalitions of Communist forces would achieve what
the United States had previously believed only the forces of the

Soviet Union could do. It seemed possible that the new Communist power might form an alliance with Ho Chi Minh, driving the French from Vietnamese territory. If this happened, all of Indochina would quickly fall into Communist hands, and the way of life most alien to America would have spread throughout the Asian world.

Recognizing the threat, the French renewed their appeals for U.S. support. They pleaded that without such aid, they might find it necessary to withdraw from Vietnam. The United States, with some reluctance, decided to lend support, but its motivation was more subtle and complex than one might at first expect. Certainly there was the issue of drawing a line in Asia, and specifically in Indochina, against the growing Communist threat. But the American desire to assist Vietnamese nationalism and independence was also a factor, and it was thought that these objectives would be achieved with greater assurance if the French were allowed to guide the process along.

Dean Acheson, secretary of state under President Truman from 1948 to 1952, defined the U.S. position as follows:

> As we saw our role in Southeast Asia, it was to help toward solving the colonial-nationalist conflict in a way that would satisfy nationalist aims and minimize the strain on our Western European allies. This meant supporting the French "presence" in the area as a guide and help to the three states in moving toward genuine independence within (for the present, at least) the French Union.[3]

Mixed with this was a careful assessment of the political dynamics of postwar Europe. Communist power was a reality in Asia; it was a very palpable reality in Europe, too. The United States felt it must do whatever was necessary to strengthen Western Europe against this threat. The only way to mount effective resistance was to strengthen the area militarily, but the French would offer strong objections if West Germany were rearmed. In exchange for France's support in Europe, therefore, the United States pledged to support the French endeavor in Indochina. The American memory was alive too. And the principal fear it contained didn't focus as much on Joseph Stalin or Mao Zedong, and certainly not on Ho Chi Minh, as on Adolf Hitler. It took Hitler less than three months to take Western Europe captive; the Japanese had become sovereign of much of Southeast Asia in even less time.

American fears were real, not fantasies. After World War II those countries that had been occupied by Russian troops one by one placed Communists in positions of authority and adopted Soviet-conceived patterns of government. The People's Republic of Albania was formed in 1946. The Socialist Republic of Romania and the Republic of Czechoslovakia came into being in 1948. Nineteen forty-nine saw the formation of the German Democratic Republic as well as the Hungarian People's Republic. The Polish People's Republic was inaugurated in 1952, and in Asia the People's Republic of China was proclaimed in 1950, two years after the Democratic People's Republic of Korea had been formed. All accepted Soviet-type rule, exhibiting devotion to Communist ideology as contained in the 1847 *Communist Manifesto* of Karl Marx and Friedrich Engels.

Nineteen fifty also witnessed the beginnings of U.S. involvement in the Korean War. It was the year of the ascendancy of Joseph McCarthy, the junior senator from Wisconsin who unmasked "Communist sympathizers" in all walks of American life. Supported by intensified feelings within the nation, fears increased that the domino theory would prove correct—that one country after another would fall into Communist control. If the process were not thwarted, Communist expansion would continue.

The Korean War made Communist China the most direct and obvious enemy of the United States, and also provided vivid illustration that both Russian and Chinese forces should be included within the category "Communist." This coalition severely diminished the status of Ho Chi Minh in American eyes. Communism was understood to be the number one evil in the world; Soviet and Chinese expansion was the primary form this evil took. Opposing this growing evil was not only the United States, but all countries in alliance with it, now member-states of the "free world." Ho Chi Minh, by virtue of his Communist identification, was the enemy too. France, by virtue of its rejection of communism, became more an ally and a partner.

Its fundamental allegiances now quite evident, the United States stopped short of becoming directly involved in the French effort in Vietnam. It did, however, provide economic and technical assistance, establishing hospitals, inoculating people against disease, and providing food, clothing and drugs to the needy. Clearly, the United States wished to strike a humanitarian pose in its support of the French, perhaps to demonstrate to the Vietnamese people that it harbored no personal ill will.

The French appealed for assistance not only to the United States, but also to others who understood the nature of the Communist threat. NATO might have been willing to help if France had been willing, in President Dwight Eisenhower's words, to make a "definite and public pledge to accord independence and the right of self-determination upon the Associated States as soon as military victory could be attained," but this France was unwilling to do.[4] Once again, a combination of European and Asian dynamics swayed U.S. foreign policy. NATO defense of Europe needed the contribution of France, but the French had been spending more and more of their military capability in the Asian theater. Eisenhower also recognized the war weariness of the French people. In seven years of fighting in Vietnam, fifty thousand French soldiers had been killed and one hundred thousand wounded. At a time when France was trying to rebuild itself following the devastations of World War II, it had spent over $5 billion fighting Ho Chi Minh.

From 1952 on the United States found it more and more difficult to support the French without actually and directly opposing the Vietnamese. The new secretary of state, John Foster Dulles, wanted to exercise a "get-tough" policy, conceding with Joseph McCarthy that the previous administration had been soft on communism. After all, the facts were there for everyone to evaluate. In the postwar years communism had advanced to envelop more and more territory, without meeting effective resistance (except in Korea). It was on the march both in Asia and in Europe. Supported by strong sentiment within the United States, Eisenhower and Dulles believed this forward motion had to be halted, then kept in check.

The continuing resistance of the French, together with their evident war weariness, only strengthened and intensified Vietnamese nationalist resolve. In 1950 Ho Chi Minh declared that while the French colonialists were "enemy number one," the nationalists were also committed to "oppose the U.S. interventionists. The deeper their interference," Ho said, "the closer our solidarity and the more vigorous our struggle." He expressed confidence that

> close solidarity between the peoples of Viet Nam, Cambodia and Laos constitutes a force capable of defeating the imperialists and the U.S. interventionists. The U.S. imperialists have failed in China, they will fail in Indochina.
>
> We are running into many difficulties, but we are bound to win.[5]

On September 2, 1950, on the fifth anniversary of Vietnamese independence, Ho explained his attitude toward the United States:

> Since the outbreak of hostilities in Viet Nam, the French government has been overthrown over a dozen times; French commanders-in-chief have been replaced five or six times; French troops have been worn down; France's finances have dwindled with every passing day. The French people's antiwar movement has spread more extensively. Our people have grown ever more united and resolute.
>
> Now the French colonialists have openly admitted that they are exhausted and cannot prolong the war unless they are helped by the U.S.A.
>
> While begging for U.S. help, they are afraid lest the Americans oust them from Indochina, as the Japanese did a few years ago.

> Ever since the war started, the Americans have done their best to help the French. But at present they go one step further by directly interfering in Viet Nam.
>
> So, apart from our principal enemy, the French colonialists, we have now another foe, the American interventionists.[6]

The crucial battle occurred in 1954 in Dienbienphu, in the very northwest corner of Vietnam. This was the city at which both sides drew firm battle lines. Each knew it would be a crucial test, that the victor could go on decisively to win the entire war. Each committed its best forces. Each was prepared to give the battle its utmost.

Ho's army won easily and dramatically. For the first time in three centuries of colonialism, Asian troops defeated Western forces in open battle, and the rest of the world soon learned that what was transpiring in the jungles was no small domestic skirmish.

The direct result of the battle at Dienbienphu was an international conference in Geneva, with the Russians, French, British, Americans, Chinese, and Vietminh nationalists participating. Following some acutely acrimonious sessions, a final agreement was hammered out. It called for a military cease-fire, the partition of the country (as in Korea) into northern and southern sections, restrictions against the imposition of new or additional military forces in the region, restrictions on both sections against forming new military alliances or providing opportunities for outsiders to establish military bases, and civil elections in two years.

On September 20, 1954, France, Great Britain, Australia, New Zealand, Thailand, the Philippines, Pakistan, and the United States formed SEATO, the Southeast Asia Treaty Organization—the Asian counterpart to NATO—one of the express purposes of which was to maintain Cambodia, Laos, and South Vietnam against Communist encroachment. The Geneva accords and the SEATO agreement encouraged the United States to take over from France the leadership role in Southeast

Asia. The twin settlements, in President Eisenhower's words,

> ended a bloody war and a serious drain on France's
> resources. More important, it saw the beginning of the
> development of better understanding between the
> western powers and the nations of Southeast Asia. It
> paved the way for a system of true cooperation
> between both in the never-ending struggle to stem the
> tide of communist expansion.[7]

But the civil war continued, almost independently of the
international dimensions, as though the Geneva accords had no
serious authority at all. The civil elections did not occur. In lieu
of these, the United States did its best to establish (in 1954) and
support the premiership of Ngo Dinh Diem, a member of one
of Vietnam's royal families, who, in the 1930s, had served Bao
Dai, the emperor, as minister of the interior. Diem had been
captured by Ho Chi Minh's forces in 1945. Ho had invited him
to join ranks with his independent government in the north,
but Diem refused, living outside the country for the next
decade. A staunch Roman Catholic, Diem was befriended by
Francis Cardinal Spellman, who helped arrange for him to
attend school in the United States, primarily at Maryknoll
seminaries, between 1951 and 1953. Spellman also introduced
Diem to leading American Catholic intellectuals, notably Mike
Mansfield, senator from Montana, and John F. Kennedy. Well-
liked and highly respected by Americans, Diem was given
considerable authority as well as financial assistance by the
Eisenhower administration. At home, his status was contested
from the first. Yet each time his tenure appeared vulnerable, he
was propped up by the money and persuasive power of the
United States and by the confidence of John Foster Dulles,
Eisenhower's secretary of state.

Tension grew between the United States and France. By
1956, the French had abandoned the country nearly completely, and the United States assumed responsibility for training the South Vietnamese army. By this time the United States
was spending close to $100 million per year for military equip-
ment for the South Vietnamese, and it also provided more than

$127 million in direct economic assistance and $17 million in technical assistance.

With such strong outside support, Diem survived the series of direct challenges that came his way, but by the early 1960s South Vietnam was enveloped in civil disturbances. Diem was never fully accepted by the Buddhist segment of the population. He lacked the charisma of Ho Chi Minh, and his close ties with the United States had also alienated a significant proportion of the populace who did not always appreciate or understand the U.S. presence. The citizenry in revolt became easy prey for the subversive activities of the North Vietnamese, under the leadership of Ho Chi Minh, whose fundamental nationalistic intentions remained firm. A strong combination of internal and external forces threatened to bring Diem's government down, but this was forestalled by the election of Diem's friend, John F. Kennedy, to the U.S. presidency in 1960.

Kennedy's hope from the beginning – indeed, from his days as a U.S. senator – was that strong leadership would emerge in South Vietnam to steer the anticolonial revolution away from domination by the Communists. He expressed himself repeatedly on this subject on the floor of the Senate. He believed that "the potential power of a free Asian nationalism" would eventually help create "an independent, anti-Communist Vietnam" with the assistance of U.S. military and economic aid. Exuding the confidence that belonged to the United States at that time, Kennedy believed that "some miracle" would occur to the benefit of the Vietnamese and the delight of the American people. He viewed President Diem as the leader who would guide a free Vietnam toward independence.[8]

The confidence of such views can be illustrated by a footnote appended to one of Kennedy's speeches by the editor of *The Strategy of Peace*, in which they are included. Allan Nevins wrote:

> Since this speech was made, the vision which it embodies has been amply justified by events. When in the summer of 1954 Vietnam was partitioned between Communist North and Nationalist South [a conception

also worthy of comment], most people feared that aggressive Red forces would soon sweep over the whole country. But the faith of friends like Senator Kennedy was actually well founded. The United States had the wisdom to grant South Vietnam about $500 million in various forms of assistance – military aid, help to refugees, and the improvement of agriculture, industry, education, and public health.

As a result, Nevins continues,

the little republic truly became what Mr. Kennedy calls it, a proving ground for democracy. It has produced in its President, Ngo Dinh Diem, one of the true statesmen of the new Asia. Peace and order have been restored, food is abundant, the economic life is troubled only by inflation, and education is improving.

In summary, "With current economic aid ot about $185 million, Vietnam is a country of which the West may feel proud, and which it should continue to protect."[9]

By the time Kennedy became President, Diem was involved in an all-out war against the forces of Ho Chi Minh. In 1961 the West witnessed the Berlin blockade and the sharp increase of avowed militancy by Nikita Khrushchev. Then there was Castro in Cuba, troubles in the Congo, and the beginnings of uprisings throughout Africa and the so-called Third World. Ho's successes against Diem's army became more numerous and impressive, and the United States responded by sending more aid. Wishing to demonstrate an attitude of toughness toward communism – no one could afford to be soft on communism – President Kennedy expanded U.S. commitments by sending in more weapons and men, and by initiating a counterinsurgency program to combat whatever psychological advantage the Vietcong had gained.

Questions about the American venture became more prevalent at home, however. Not only was the war not going according to the U.S. plan, but in light of the evident corruption and unpopularity of the Diem regime, U.S. policies were becoming more difficult to defend. President Kennedy, encouraged by Senator Mike Mansfield and others, considered liquidating the U.S. presence in 1963, and might have recommended the same, apparently, had he not been worried that the citizenry would understand this to represent a soft-on-communism stance. In the meantime, Buddhist leaders were demonstrating against the Diem government, and the pictures of burning monks carried in the Western press dramatized the conflict to those outside. Fourteen hundred Buddhists were arrested, increasing anti-Diem sentiment both at home and abroad.

In November 1963 Diem was assassinated, just three weeks before John F. Kennedy suffered the same fate. When the new President, Lyndon B. Johnson, took office, the situation in South Vietnam was more precarious than ever. Johnson sensed that the American cause there might be lost totally. Wishing to push for a comprehensive domestic social program, President Johnson found the conflict in Vietnam an unnecessary debilitation and established a successor government to the Diem regime, with only lukewarm support. General William Westmoreland, a veteran of both World War II and the Korean War, was placed in charge of U.S. troops in South Vietnam, and the new President announced to Ho Chi Minh that continued interference in the affairs of South Vietnam – a clear violation of the Geneva accords – would be met by decisive U.S. reaction.

The occasion for direct confrontation presented itself in the late summer, on August 2, 1964, before Lyndon Johnson had served a full year of his presidency. On that day three North Vietnamese patrol boats fired at a U.S. destroyer in international waters about thirty miles off the coast of North Vietnam. The official announcement from the U.S. State Department said simply:

> While on routine patrol in international waters at 4:06 A.M., Eastern Daylight Time, the United States destroyer *Maddox* underwent an unprovoked attack by three PT-type boats at latitude 19-40 north, longitude 106-34 east, in Tonkin Gulf. The attacking boats launched three torpedoes and used 37-mm. gunfire.

On August 4, President Johnson ordered retaliatory action. Explaining his decision to the American people by television, the President said that the U.S. military was attacking on a limited basis with conventional weapons in order to destroy the North Vietnamese gunboats.

> In the larger sense, this new act of aggression aimed directly at our own forces again brings home to all of us in the United States the importance of the struggle for peace and security in Southeast Asia.
>
> Aggression by terror against the peaceful villages of South Vietnam has now been joined by open aggression on the high seas against the United States of America.
>
> The determination of all Americans to carry out our full commitment to the people and to the Government of South Vietnam will be redoubled by this outrage. Yet our response for the present will be limited and fitting.
>
> We Americans know – although others appear to forget – the risk of spreading conflict. We still seek no wider war.
>
> I have instructed the Secretary of State to make this position totally clear to friends and to adversaries and, indeed, to all.
>
> I have instructed Ambassador Stevenson to raise this matter immediately and urgently before the Security Council of the United Nations.[10]

On Wednesday, August 5, Ambassador Adlai Stevenson explained U.S. action to the United Nations Security Council. Confirming that the United States had destroyed twenty-five patrol boats and had bombed naval craft and oil storage depots in a five-hour raid along one hundred miles of North Vietnamese coastline, he declared, "We are in Southeast Asia to help our friends preserve their own opportunity to be free of imported terror, or alien assassination managed by the North Vietnam Communists based in Hanoi and backed by the Chinese Communists from Peking."[11] Stevenson termed the United States action "an act of self-defense" authorized by international law and the United Nations charter.

On the same day, Secretary of State Dean Rusk commented in New York that "the other side got a sting out of this. If they do it again, they'll get another sting."[12] And Robert S.

McNamara, secretary of defense, announced that the United States was rushing fighting men, planes, and ships to Southeast Asia to reinforce its presence there.

Also on August 5, 1964, workers in Jackson, Mississippi, identified three bodies found buried deep inside a cattle-pond dam as those of missing civil rights workers. The bodies were encased in black plastic bags. The coincidence of such events enabled the citizenry to speak of them as though they belonged together. It was the power of the conjunction that stimulated the antiwar activists.

The next day, August 6, Senator Wayne Morse of Oregon spoke passionately on the floor of the Senate in opposition to a resolution requested by President Johnson to approve "all necessary measures to repel any armed attack against the United States and to prevent further aggression" against the nations of the Southeast Asia Treaty Organization. Morse called the resolution "a predated declaration of war," adding that the United States was the real "provocateur" in the incident. Senator George McGovern of South Dakota was willing to concur, stating that he was puzzled and baffled "as to why a little state such as North Vietnam should seek a deliberate naval conflict with the United States." Morse followed: "If Senators want my opinion, a 'snow-job' is being done on us by the Pentagon and the State Department." He pleaded that the proper action for the U.S. government to take was to place the entire matter before the United Nations. He was unalterably opposed to any resolution "which takes the form of military action to expand the war or that encourages our puppets in Saigon to expand the war."[13]

But in spite of such protestations, the House of Representatives voted 416–0 to pass the resolution requested by the President. The same measure passed in the Senate, 88–2, with only Senators Morse and Ernest Gruening of Alaska dissenting.

On August 7, Andrei Gromyko, the Soviet foreign minister, assured the North Vietnamese government in Hanoi of the diplomatic backing of the Soviet Union. He added, "The Soviet government has demanded that the United States should immediately stop military operations against the Democratic Republic of Vietnam."[14]

Also on August 7, 1964, Robert Kennedy declared that he was considering running for the U.S. Senate seat in New York. Governor Nelson Rockefeller's office announced that he had no intention of stumping for the Goldwater ticket, either inside or outside New York State, and the U.S. House of Representatives approved President Johnson's antipoverty bill. It was a momentous day.

By 1964, several strong incentives for direct U.S. military involvement in Vietnam had been fused. Together they came to characterize American foreign policy in Indochina and throughout the world.

In the first place, the United States ordinarily wanted to encourage those nations and peoples seeking emancipation from colonial rule. As Ho stated in his speech on Vietnamese Independence Day, this was the very situation that had given birth to America. But such an attitude became problematic when crucial situations arose, since the United States had always found its choicest friends and closest allies among the colonial powers – specifically, Great Britain and France. Thus postwar U.S. foreign policy had to walk an exceedingly delicate path. In Vietnam, friendship with France was accorded priority over support of nationalism, which led to direct confrontation.

At the same time, the postwar period saw the rise of the United States as the strongest country, the leader, of the "free world." North America had not been ravaged as the lands of most of the other participants had been. Though the United States suffered great losses, it was able to recover very quickly, and the fact that it was the sole possessor of nuclear weaponry gave it a pre-eminence that it had never enjoyed before. This new status carried large responsibilities for postwar reconstruction and political realignments. Thus, it was to be expected that wherever American influence reached, including South Vietnam, American models of government and capitalism would become established.

The United States could not presume to spread its influence without encountering opposition, however. The Soviet

Union had also been a victor in the war, and had brought the nations it had occupied within its political, economic, and ideological orbit. The contest was under way from the very day the Germans surrendered to the Allies in 1945, and every U.S. decision had to be weighed in full awareness of its bearing on this fundamental world contest.

American decision-makers were thus under pressure to try to honor at least three criteria in executing foreign policy. First, they wished to protect the friendship of those seeking freedom from oppression. Second, they wished to maintain the fabric of military and economic cooperation in the "free world" by remaining supportive of France, Great Britain, and U.S. allies in NATO and SEATO. Third, they wished to build, then sustain, clear advantages over the Soviet Union.

The United States would have looked good in all situations if the three objectives had been compatible, but more often than not they were in conflict. Faced with mutually exclusive alternatives, the foreign-policy-makers were forced to set priorities, and in the reshuffling, the desire to achieve supremacy over the Soviet Union gained prominence. Perhaps there were no other effective ways of proceeding, but as a consequence, American perceptions of U.S. motivation were revised. In time U.S. alliances with peoples seeking emancipation were revised too. The Soviets were viewed as colonizers, the instruments of oppression, and those needing emancipation were those in bondage to Soviet rule. Communist ideology, rather than colonialist ambitions, was understood to be the power that kept peoples under dominion, for everyone knew that the Soviets had embarked on a program of world domination.

Hence, when the postwar U.S. Presidents, from Harry Truman to Gerald Ford, were forced into crucial and sometimes agonizing decisions concerning the struggle in Vietnam, they characteristically selected opposition to Soviet power as the priority to protect. They could do nothing, over the long haul, that might be construed as soft on communism. When the crunch came in Vietnam, the United States decided to be anti-Communist, and thus anti-Ho, rather than to involve itself in other ways in a previously colonized nation's striving for inde-

pendence. The justification was that Ho was in direct ideological league with the United States' chief rival, and thus with the
power center representing the gravest threat to U.S. security
and to the well-being of the "free world."

While this attitude made sense at certain levels of abstrac-
tion, it was less useful within the drama at hand. In the first
place, Ho (unlike Hitler) did not seem intent on annexing any
additional territory once the situation in Vietnam was rectified.
Second, only by elaborate conjectures – the domino theory, or
the fear that Red China was the real force involved – could Ho
ever be taken seriously as a threat to the United States. But
unless some such allusions or equations could be defended, the
United States had little reason to exercise a strong sense of
proprietorship over the contested territories of Indochina.

In short, during the period from 1945 to 1965, with the
South Vietnamese showing ambivalent resolve and the United
States being called upon increasingly to exercise leadership
within the international world, Vietnam became more and
more of a stumbling block and scandal to American aspirations.
The defense of the American involvement given by the nation's
leaders contained too many inconsistencies to be persuasive.
When the inconsistencies were identified, and the issues they
masked debated, the real enemy became internalized in very
little time. Once this transposition occurred, increased and
intensified military efforts simply added to the fire.

Before anyone quite knew how it happened, the primary
issue was both Vietnam and the American character, for these
had become virtually interchangeable. This preoccupation distinguished the Vietnamese conflict from the understanding of
the nature of war that had been incorporated in American
experience since at least the beginning of the twentieth
century. In the two world wars, the enemy was clearly identifiable. Military battles concerned the taking of real land, measur-
able geographical space. Furthermore, the United States had
been forced to become involved because it had been attacked.
The only decision the leadership had to make was whether to
respond to direct threats to our security and possessions. For

example, once Pearl Harbor had been bombed and strafed, President Franklin D. Roosevelt had no great difficulty in rallying the nation or tapping its internal resolve. All he needed to do was to direct American enthusiasm and patriotism against an enemy everyone opposed. Even the Korean War carried United Nations sanctions, and thus the leadership could appeal to a broad basis of support.

But Vietnam was different. Here the enemy was more difficult to identify, and patriotic fervor, if elicited, could barely be sustained. The nation was involved in war, but only some of that war's intensity was being directed outward. In 1950 Senator McCarthy was pointing patriotic vengeance not as much toward Russia, China, or North Vietnam as toward Communist sympathizers within the nation. By 1965 those who took to the streets, in no way sympathetic to Joe McCarthy's cause, were also rallying against those in power within the government. As ironical as it might seem, judged from the earlier perspective, returning combat veterans also joined in the mass protests against the leadership of the country as the Vietnam War ground on into irresolution.

In the aftermath, with ideological assurances up for grabs, what Robert Lifton calls "the crisis in authority and mentorship" became monumental.[15] No one could be quite certain of being able to find the "real America" until a certain segment of the populace, later called the New Right, produced "I have found it" bumper stickers more than a decade later. And those who found it could hardly experience it except in relation to the impact of the war. It was in military terms, and with evangelical zeal, that the rediscovered patriotism was expressed.

4. Exit from Eden

"We are in the position of a man who has been attacked by a swarm of bees, and who can defend himself only with a submachine gun. By the law of averages, he is going to hit a bee from time to time, but he is not going to have a very effective defense."
— HANS MORGENTHAU

THE SCENE IS Sproul Plaza in Berkeley, California, on September 30, 1964, in the midst of the Lyndon Johnson–Barry Goldwater presidential contest. Here a graduate student in philosophy, Mario Savio, led five hundred students in protest because the dean's office had summoned five students for questioning in connection with the violation of new University of California rules regarding free speech in the Hyde Park area on Bancroft Way. Savio and the others protested that all had broken the new rules, not only the five who had been summoned; hence all should receive punishment equally.

The issue? Not the war in Vietnam, even though the event is remembered as the first great civil protest against American military involvement in Southeast Asia. No, the primary issue was civil rights, specifically the hiring practices of the *Oakland Tribune*, which Savio and his associates had discovered to be racially discriminatory. The protestors, some of whom had spent part of the previous summer working for civil rights in Alabama and Mississippi, were sensitive to the situation of black and other minority citizens in the East Bay cities, and knew such people were discriminated against when they applied for jobs, not only with the *Tribune*. And they were speaking out.

The *Tribune* was Senator William Knowland's paper. Being tough on communism, the senator had utilized it to call attention to the growing menace, both abroad and internally. When an executive of the newspaper learned of the focus and object of the students' concerns, he telephoned the administrative offices of the University of California to request that the free speech area be closed. The university administration responded by announcing on September 21, 1964 – the first full day of classes for the 1964–65 academic year – that the rights of free speech would be upheld but under some new restrictions: There was to be no advocacy, no fund-raising, no recruitment, and nothing that directly advanced political or social causes. Of course the students did not accept the administrative ruling. When they flouted it openly, the stage was set for the demonstrations on September 30.

The following day more students appeared in Sproul Plaza. When they failed to disperse, the university called upon its campus police to establish order. Exercising the methods of nonviolence which many had been practicing in civil-rights demonstrations in the South earlier in the year, some of the students fell limp, and some surrounded the police car that was there to carry off the primary troublemakers. For thirty-two hours they held the car captive, using its roof as a rostrum for their speeches.

The next day, Clark Kerr, president of the university, reiterated the "free speech" policy. This time the task of establishing law and order was given to approximately one thousand policemen, including some campus police, State Highway Patrol officers, city police, and sheriff units from nearby counties. The force was large enough to maintain order, but the conflict was not resolved.

University leaders met with the leaders of the protest movement. On November 23, President Kerr threatened Savio and a second student leader with expulsion; on December 2, after the Thanksgiving break, some six thousand students turned out to support Savio. Fifteen hundred proceeded to enter the university's administrative offices, where eight hundred were arrested. Classes stopped. Students declared themselves to be on strike, and many of the faculty rallied to their support.

On December 7, in the Greek theater on campus, President Kerr addressed the student body and faculty and pleaded for collective equanimity. As he finished his speech, Savio came forward to announce that a mass rally was scheduled, but before he could speak he was seized by police. Thousands of students started to come forward to rescue their leader. But Clark intervened and allowed Savio to speak, and direct physical confrontation was avoided. The next day the faculty voted to meet the demands of the Free Speech Movement, as Savio's group was called. The decision was not even close: 824 in favor, 115 opposed. No restrictions were to be imposed on political activity on the campus.

The campus was quieter, at least for a time. Christmas vacation intervened, and the students were busy during much of January preparing for final examinations. Yet the situation had not been fully resolved.

In February 1965 the national civil-rights movement was still emerging. Having won a clear mandate from the electorate in November, President Johnson was determined to push the legislation of his announced Great Society. His intention was to bring the Vietnam conflict to successful resolution as promptly and decisively as possible so that attention would not be deflected from his domestic goals.

But the President's action in escalating American involvement in the war became counterproductive. On Sunday, February 7, Johnson confirmed that the United States had carried out an effective bombing mission over North Vietnam. He indicated that forty-nine carrier-based fighter planes had bombed and strafed barracks and staging areas of the Vietcong guerrillas in the vicinity of Donghoi, just north of the border separating North and South Vietnam. Premier Aleksei Kosygin of the Soviet Union was visiting Hanoi at the time, and pledged that Moscow would assist North Vietnam against any nation that encroached upon its territory. President Johnson responded by reiterating that the United States sought "no wider war," but warned that such a course depended upon the intentions of the North Vietnamese "aggressors."

On February 9, in his column in the *Washington Post*, Walter Lippmann called the war in Vietnam the "war that cannot be won on the ground where it is being fought." But on

February 11 the attacks continued, when twenty U.S. jet
fighters accompanied by even more South Vietnamese planes
attacked North Vietnam and twenty-one American soldiers lost
their lives. Hanoi claimed that four American aircraft had been
downed; the United States responded that there had been only
three. Both sides agreed that an American pilot had been taken
captive.

On February 12, Senator Frank Church of Idaho spoke at
length on the floor of the Senate about the roots of the difficulty. Influenced by Walter Lippmann's editorial, Church
observed that the United States had become "grossly over-
extended in regions where we have no primary vital interest."
Elaborating, he said:

> We have come to treat "Communism," regardless of
> what form it may take in any given country, as the
> enemy. We fancy ourselves as guardians of the "free"
> world, though most of it is not free, and never has
> been. We seek to immunize this world against further
> Communist infection through massive injections of
> American aid, and, wherever necessary, through
> direct American intervention. Such a vast undertaking
> has at least two defects: first, it exceeds our national
> capability; second, among the newly-emerging
> nations, where the specter of Western imperialism is
> dreaded more than Communism, such a policy can be
> self-defeating. As a seasoned, friendly foreign diplo-
> mat recently put it: "The United States is getting in-
> volved in situations where no one – not even a nation
> of saints – would be welcome . . ."
> To avoid this, we must understand that, for most
> Africans and Asians, our concept of self-government
> and individual freedom is totally unreal, having never
> been experienced. In many, if not most, of these emer-
> gent lands, it is capitalism, not Communism, which is
> the ugly word.[1]

But on the same day, February 12, one hundred and sixty
U.S. and South Vietnamese planes attacked military bases in
the north. A State Department bulletin confirmed that the air
strikes had occurred, in response to "continued acts of aggression by Communist Vietcong under the direction and with the
support of the Hanoi regime." On the same day, the White

House tried to maintain a distinction between "outright war against North Vietnam" and "retaliatory air strikes" of the kind that were being ordered more frequently by the military command.

On February 15 the *Daily Cal*, the student newspaper in Berkeley, carried an editorial which reported that "the campus and the entire nation have recently been immersed in conversation about the confusing situation in North and South Vietnam." The next day one hundred University of California students, led by Art Goldberg, Savio's close friend and associate, marched in protest to the U.S. Army terminal in Oakland.

On February 25 U.S. air power was unleashed once again over North Vietnam. The State Department announced that the massive air strikes had been made at the request of the government of South Vietnam. U Thant, secretary-general of the United Nations, said that he favored informal negotiations for the establishment of a stable government in South Vietnam as well as U.S. withdrawal of forces from Southeast Asia. The State Department responded the following day with a white paper admitting that U.S. policy in Vietnam had shifted.

On March 1, eighty faculty members of the University of California at Berkeley were among those signing a full-page ad in the *New York Times* protesting U.S. involvement in Vietnam. The next weeks saw repetitions of similar activities. There were antiwar speeches in Sproul Plaza, continued marches on the Army terminal in Oakland, arrests of students, dramatic burnings of draft cards, teach-ins concerning the dynamics of the war and the techniques of nonviolent protest, and, on May 15, an antiwar rally attended by more than fifteen thousand people.

What was transpiring in Berkeley was also spreading to other campuses and civic locations. Significantly, most of these demonstrations began not as protests against U.S. involvement in Indochina, but in dissatisfaction with local situations. Yet most of the frustration came eventually to focus on the war, the common denominator through which the protests here and there became welded into a united front.

The Free Speech Movement in Berkeley was brought into being by heightened collective sensitivity to rampant racial discrimination. Senator William Knowland and the *Oakland Tribune* were natural targets because of the hypocrisy their racist policies implied. But the same fervor was behind the growing resistance toward U.S. involvement in the Asian war. It is significant that when the movement became radicalized, its furor was directed not against conservatives, but against liberals — against Clark Kerr, the guarantor of the rights and privileges of the Enlightenment, and against Lyndon Johnson, the architect of the Great Society, whose ambition was to realize concretely the founding fathers' aspirations for equal opportunity under the law for all citizens.

Indeed, for a time at least, President Johnson defended U.S. policy toward Vietnam on the basis of the liberal creed, which was dictating domestic economic and social policy as well. Speaking to an audience at Johns Hopkins University on April 7, 1965, and particularly in answer to the question of why the United States had undertaken military action in Vietnam, the President said: "We fight because we must fight if we are to live in a world where every country can shape its own destiny. And only in such a world will our own freedom be finally secure."

On the same occasion the President sketched in the larger perspective:

> Over this war, and all Asia, is another reality: the deepening shadow of Communist China. The rulers in Hanoi are urged on by Peking. This is a regime which has destroyed freedom in Tibet, attacked India, and been condemned by the United Nations for aggression in Korea. It is a nation which is helping the forces of violence in almost every continent. The contest in Vietnam is part of a wider pattern of aggressive purpose.

Again Johnson asked, "Why are we in Vietnam?" The reply: 'Because we have a promise to keep" to the people of South Vietnam, "to strengthen world order."

> Around the globe, from Berlin to Thailand, are
> people whose well-being rests, in part, on the belief
> that they can count on us if they are attacked. To leave
> Vietnam to its fate would shake the confidence of all
> these people in the value of American commitment,
> the value of America's word.

"We are there because there are great stakes in the balance," the
President explained.

> The central lesson of our time is that the appetite of
> aggression is never satisfied. To withdraw from one
> battlefield means only to prepare for the next. We
> must say in Southeast Asia, as we did in Europe, in the
> words of the Bible: "Hitherto shalt thou come, but no
> further."

Pledging to withdraw as soon as "the bright and necessary day
of peace" came, the President suggested that the people of
North Vietnam "want what their neighbors also desire: food for
their hunger, health for their bodies and a chance to learn,
progress for their country, and an end to the bondage of mate-
rial misery." After the hostilities end, the United Nations might
assist a "plan for cooperation in increased development," a plan
that sounds very much like an extension of the ambitions of the
Great Society.

> The task is nothing less than to enrich the hopes and
> existence of more than a hundred million people. And
> there is much to be done.
> The vast Mekong River can provide food and water
> on a scale to dwarf even our own TVA [Tennessee
> Valley Authority].

Then came the reiteration of the liberal creed:

> For centuries, nations have struggled among each
> other. But we dream of a world where disputes are
> settled by law and reason. And we will try to make it
> so.
> For most of history men have hated and killed one
> another in battle. But we dream of an end to war. And
> we will try to make it so.

> For all existence most men have lived in poverty,
> threatened by hunger. But we dream of a world where
> all are fed and charged with hope. And we will make
> it so.

The liberal creed was supported by and infused with much
personal religious feeling: "Every night before I turn out the
lights to sleep, I ask myself this question: Have I done everything I can to help unite the world, to try to bring peace and
hope to all the peoples of the world? Have I done enough?"

As the President confessed, he was reminded of certain
Biblical passages:

> We may well be living in the time foretold many
> years ago when it was said, "I call heaven and earth to
> record this day against you, that I have set before you
> life and death, blessing and cursing: therefore choose
> life, that both thou and thy seed shall live."
> This generation of the world must choose: destroy
> or build, kill or aid, hate or understand.
> We can do these things on a scale never dreamed of
> before.
> We will choose life. And so doing we will prevail
> over the enemies within man, and over the natural
> enemies of all mankind.[2]

All of this—the analysis, the creed, the prayer, and the
homiletic injunction—was offered as a rationale for United
States military involvement in Vietnam.

The white paper issued by the State Department less than
two months before explained the matter somewhat differently.
Published to explain the shift in U.S. policy, the document
carries the title "Aggression from the North" and the subtitle
"The Record of North Viet-Nam's Campaign to Conquer South
Viet-Nam," and features a quotation from President Johnson's
February 17 address: "Our purpose in Vietnam is to join in the
defense and protection of freedom of a brave people who are
under attack that is controlled and directed from outside their
country."[3]

The introduction to the document provides a chronicle of
how the people of South Vietnam are fighting for their lives

against a "brutal campaign of terror and armed attack inspired, directed, supplied, and controlled by the Communist regime in Hanoi." Calling this "flagrant aggression," the document proceeds to distinguish U.S. hostilities, which may seem to carry some resemblance, from North Vietnamese actions. One fundamental difference is that in Vietnam, "a Communist government has set out deliberately to conquer a sovereign people in a neighboring state." "To achieve its end," this government "has used every resource of its own government to carry out its carefully planned program of concealed aggression," much like the aggression of the North Koreans in 1950. Both are linked to the expansionism of Communist China, which is said to be the chief supplier of weaponry to both. In view of such aggressive acts, which threaten the security of the "free world," the United States has become involved only in response to "the appeals of the Government of the Republic of Vietnam for help in this defense of the freedom and independence of its land and people."

The white paper also identifies the kinds of weapons North Vietnam used (manufactured both in China and the Soviet Union) and the supply routes by which it carried ammunition into battle areas, and provides character sketches of some of the North Vietnamese military leaders and combat veterans. Scattered throughout are references to Ho Chi Minh. The paper cites a speech in which Ho spoke of the necessity "to step up the socialist revolution in the North and, at the same time, to step up the national democratic people's revolution in the South," and quotes from an article he wrote in 1959 for the newspaper *Red Flag* (the Communist Party's official newspaper in Belgium), in which he said, "We are building socialism in Viet-Nam, but we are building it in only one part of the country, while in the other part we still have to direct and bring to a close the middle-class democratic and anti-imperialist revolution." Such citations ostensibly demonstrate that the subversive activities of Ho's forces belong to a deliberate, calculated plan to create more havoc in South Vietnam, part of the more comprehensive Communist intention to take over as much of the world as it can.

Significantly, the white paper's point of historical orientation is 1954, and it appeals to the Geneva accords of the same
year. It accuses the Vietnamese Communists of planning to
take over all former French territory in Southeast Asia, and to
have been duplicitously working at the very moment they were
signing agreements with their adversaries.

The white paper makes no reference whatever to Vietnamese history prior to 1954. It offers not the slightest hint that
what looked like communist aggression was a serious attempt
to liberate the homeland from foreign rule; nor is there any
acknowledgment that colonialism may have been a factor.
Nothing is said about the period of French domination or about
the Japanese occupation during World War II. No reference is
made to the partnership between Ho Chi Minh's forces and the
United States in helping to rid the country of the Japanese
invaders.

South Vietnamese interests are viewed in the same light,
that is, from a perspective framed by the Geneva accords of
1954. Because of flagrant North Vietnamese violations of the
treaty, the government in Saigon was forced to seek the help of
the United States. Because of its concern for the freedom of a
potentially oppressed people, the United States had been
watching the situation closely.

> Though it has been apparent for years that the
> regime in Hanoi was conducting a campaign of con-
> quest against South Vietnam, the Government in
> Saigon and the Government of the United States both
> hoped that the danger could be met within South Viet-
> nam itself. The hope that any widening of the conflict
> might be avoided was stated frequently.

Not until 1961 did South Vietnam specifically request the assistance of the United States, and in response to blatant North
Vietnamese activity "air strikes have been made against some
of the military assembly points and supply bases from which
North Viet-Nam is conducting its aggression against the South."

The paper concludes with the statement that though the
North Vietnamese had repeatedly violated the peace agreements and thus were threatening the stability of the entire

Southeast Asian area, the United States was doing nothing more than taking "its place beside the South Vietnamese in their defensive struggle."

> The United States seeks no territory, no military bases, no favored position. But we have learned the meaning of aggression elsewhere in the postwar world, and we have met it.

Then comes the final assurance:

> If peace can be restored in South Viet-Nam, the United States will be ready at once to reduce its military involvement. But it will not abandon friends who want to remain free. It will do what must be done to help them. The choice now between peace and continued and increasingly destructive conflict is one for the authorities in Hanoi to make.

Ho Chi Minh's response was delivered as an address to the second session of the Third National Assembly of his government.

> Like a thief crying "Stop thief," the U.S. imperialist aggressors have impudently slandered North Viet Nam as "committing aggression" against South Viet Nam. Saboteurs of peace and of the Geneva Agreements, they brazenly claim that it is because they wish to "restore peace" and "defend the Geneva Agreements" that they are sending U.S. troops to our country to kill and destroy.
>
> They are devastating our land and massacring our people, yet they hypocritically boast that they will grant one billion dollars to the people of Viet Nam and other Southeast Asian countries to "develop their economy and improve their livelihood."
>
> The "escalation" plan which the U.S. imperialists are now trying to carry out in North Viet Nam is also doomed to failure. Even though they may bring in hundreds of thousands more U.S. troops, and strive to drag more troops of their satellites into this criminal war, our army and people are resolved to fight and defeat them.

Then Ho provided some assurances of his own.

We love peace but we are not afraid of war. We are determined to drive away the U.S. aggressors to defend the freedom, independence and territorial integrity of our fatherland . . .

Our people are very grateful to, and highly value the fraternal solidarity and devoted assistance of the socialist countries—especially the Soviet Union and China—and the people on all continents who are actively supporting our struggle against the U.S. imperialist aggressors—the most cruel enemy of mankind.

Indicating that he was well aware of the protests occurring within the United States—he had witnessed the same phenomenon in France prior to the battle of Dienbienphu—Ho Chi Minh showed his conciliatory side.

The American people have been deceived by the propaganda of their government which has extorted billions of dollars from them to pour into the war. Thousands of their sons have been tragically killed or wounded on the Viet Nam battlefields thousands of miles away from the United States. At present, many organizations and personalities in the United States are urging their government to stop its unjust war at once and withdraw U.S. troops from South Viet Nam immediately. Our people are determined to drive away the U.S. imperialists, their sworn enemy. Yet, we always express friendship toward progressive American people.[4]

But the situation had become rigidified, and the events of the war simply steamrolled under their own momentum. By July 1965 it was apparent that the United States was gearing itself for a major confrontation on the Asian mainland. Protests on the campuses became more frequent and pointed, and various U.S. senators (notably William Fulbright of Arkansas and George McGovern of South Dakota) made formal addresses critical of the U.S. involvement. The ballads of the day, whether by the Beatles, Bob Dylan, Joni Mitchell, or Joan Baez, carried the same message, and the force of their lyrics was matched by the poetry of Allen Ginsberg, Lawrence Ferlinghetti, Kenneth Rexroth, and others who had been touched by Buddhist religious sensibilities.

While the words of both songs and poems spoke of peace, gentleness, expanded self-awareness, and global and even cosmic harmony, the war rhetoric intensified and the attitudes of official Hanoi and Washington became all the more bellicose and uncompromising. More and more often President Johnson spoke of ridding Vietnam of "the ravages of the Communist marauders" so that some of the objectives of the Great Society might be effected there. In a conference in Manila in October 1965, he met with General Thieu and Prime Minister Ky of South Vietnam, President Park Chung Hee of Korea, Prime Minister Harold Holt of Australia, and Prime Minister Thonom Kittikachorn of Thailand, and updated and reiterated SEATO aspirations for Vietnam, stating that the area was to be free from aggression and outside interference so that hunger, illiteracy, and disease could be conquered. Later the President observed that "if there was a Johnson doctrine, these were its cornerstones—opposition to aggression; war against poverty, illiteracy, and disease; economic, social, and cultural cooperation on a regional basis; and reconciliation and peace."[5] He particularly liked the final paragraph of the agreements signed at the Manila conference:

> We do not threaten the sovereignty or territorial integrity of our neighbors, whatever their ideological alignment. We ask only that this be reciprocated. The quarrels and ambitions of ideology and the painful frictions arising from national fears and grievances should belong to the past. Aggression rooted in them must not succeed. We must play our full part in creating an environment in which reconciliation becomes possible, for in the modern world men and nations have no choice but to learn to live together as brothers.[6]

Johnson commented in his autobiography, *The Vantage Point: Perspectives of the Presidency,* that this statement "summed up what I wanted to see take shape in Asia. These were the goals I wanted to help achieve in every region and on every continent."[7]

Ho Chi Minh's reply was predictable: that the United States had intervened in the affairs of Vietnam, menacing the people's independence, endangering the peace in Asia and throughout the world, and that the real U.S. intention was to transform South Vietnam into an American colony and American military base.

So the quarrel degenerated. Each side accused the other of being the aggressor; each charged the other with forcing its will upon a reluctant people. Believing in the dictates of the Declaration of Independence, each had to paint its opponent as an imperialist determined for reasons of self-interest to frustrate the process by which an oppressed people legitimately seeks freedom. And as the rhetoric persisted, so did the fighting and the growing discontent at home.

Lyndon Johnson's exit from the scene was voluntary. On March 31, 1968, he unexpectedly announced: "I shall not seek, and I will not accept, the nomination of my party for another term as your President." This, he later confessed, was directed toward bringing the frustrating situation in Vietnam to a successful and early resolution.

> By renouncing my candidacy, I expressed a fervent wish that problems that had resisted solution would now yield to resolution. I wanted Hanoi to know that Lyndon Johnson was not using this new move toward peace as a bid for personal political gain. [He believed his withdrawal demonstrated that the desire for peace far transcended partisan political ambitions.] Maybe now, with this clearest possible evidence of our sincerity thrown into the balance, North Vietnam would come forward and agree to a dialogue – a genuine communication dedicated to peace.

He also hoped that the decision would bring an end to the protest marches and domestic disorder within the nation.

> Those who doubted me and disliked me, those who had fought my struggle to achieve justice for men and women who had for so long suffered injustice, might now be willing to adjust their rigid views and seek to fashion a workable formula for peace in the streets.[8]

The hostilities didn't end, but intensified more. During the same fateful year, 1968, the nation mourned and the world watched the assassinations of Martin Luther King, Jr., and Senator Robert Kennedy, the open rebellion and riots in Chicago during the Democratic National Convention, and the election of Richard Nixon and Spiro Agnew. The year began, on January 30, with the now famous Tet Offensive, during which a team of Vietcong soldiers blasted a large hole in the wall surrounding the U.S. Embassy in Saigon and held their position within the American compound for more than six hours. The United States, it seemed, had met its match. Ho Chi Minh's forces were difficult to defeat, and the waves of self-doubt and self-criticism increased all the more at home and among the forces the nation had sent ostensibly to quell Communist aggression abroad.

President Nixon adopted the get-tough policy so characteristic of those who believe our way of life is diametrically opposed to the Communist way of life, yet his fundamental intention was to end the war honorably. He judged that previous military force had been ineffective because it had been utilized in an indecisive manner. He appealed to "the silent majority" of Americans who wished not to be humiliated by the North Vietnamese.

As he did so, he was instructed by the new secretary of state, Henry Kissinger, who thought that

> Vietnam was not the cause of our difficulties but a symptom. We were in a period of painful adjustment to a profound transformation of global politics; we were being forced to come to grips with the tension between our history and our new necessities. For two centuries, America's participation in the world seemed to oscillate between overinvolvement and withdrawal, between expecting too much of our power and being ashamed of it, between optimistic exuberance and frustration with the ambiguities of an imperfect world.

Kissinger believed that "the deepest cause of our national unease was the realization – as yet dimly perceived – that we were becoming like other nations in the need to recognize that our power, while vast, had limits." He explained further:

> Our resources were no longer infinite in relation to our problems; instead we had to set priorities, both intellectual and material. In the Fifties and Sixties we had attempted ultimate solutions to specific problems; now our challenge was to shape a world and an American role to which we were permanently committed, which could no longer be sustained by the illusion that our exertions had a terminal point.

Behind it all, according to Kissinger, lay "the long-term problem of our relationship with the Soviet Union in the thermonuclear age, which would soon produce more ambiguous challenges."[9]

Many of America's leading intellectuals had come to similar conclusions. Arthur Schlesinger, Jr., for example, found the root of the nation's difficulties in the posture of "Stimsonianism," which he described as

> the view that an orderly world requires a single durable structure of world security, which must everywhere be protected against aggression; if aggression were permitted to go unpunished in one place, this, by infection, would lead to a general destruction of the system of world order.

Schlesinger had in mind Secretary of State Henry Stimson's reaction to the Japanese invasion of Manchuria in 1931—a reaction that gave rise to the principle of collective security, which was illustrated too in the framework of the League of Nations. In more modern dress, the same principle guided the foreign policies of the Eisenhower, Kennedy, and Johnson administrations. "McGeorge and William Bundy and Dean Rusk are, in a sense, the personal executors of the Stimsonian tradition. They argued conscientiously and powerfully for its overextension to Vietnam."

Schlesinger believed that Stimsonianism was complemented and supported by a kind of "liberal evangelism," whose genesis he traced:

> Because of the tremendous power vacuums created by the war, America and Russia appeared for a

moment in history after 1945 to be the world's two superpowers. At the same time, the phenomenon of Stalinism gave rise to an American anticommunism which rightly saw communism as a relatively unified world movement directed from a single center. For many people in the 1940s this necessary and correct anticommunism hardened into a series of conditioned reflexes which continued to guide their thoughts after communism itself was beginning to be transformed under the stress of nationalism. For example, when Vice-President Hubert Humphrey in October 1967 declared that the threat to peace was militant, aggressive Asian communism with headquarters in Peking, of which the action in Vietnam was the current and immediate expression, he was talking from the conditioned reflexes of the liberal evangelism of the forties.

Schlesinger confessed that he had been an advocate of both principles and that he had been acting in good faith. But the Vietnam experience had chastened him.

. . . One must now recognize the measure of the tragedy we got into in Vietnam, a tragedy that is all the more poignant because of its conceptual roots—the noble traditions of Stimsonianism and of liberal evangelism—both of which, in times past, expressed some of the best moments in American foreign policy.[10]

James C. Thomson, Jr., an East Asian specialist in the State Department and White House from 1961 to 1966, when U.S. policy on Vietnam was being formulated, echoed Schlesinger's convictions:

My hope, out of all of this tragedy, is that America will somehow be a chastened nation in the aftermath of Vietnam. This is the first war we have watched so closely on television. This is a war about which we have more volumes of printed literature than any previous war. The record of our failure is available to the general public as never before. I hope we will go through a chastening period in which we will be knocked out of our grandiosity, a period in which we will see the self-righteous, illusory quality of that vision of ourselves offered by the high Washington official who said that while other nations have "interests," the United States has "a sense of responsibility."

If Vietnam can result in a reduction of grandiosity on our part, it should likewise result in a discovery that we are, in one sense, quite similar to everyone else—we have our own problems . . . But it should also make us discover that, in another sense, we are also very unlike others and that in this highly diverse world there are diverse routes to development.[11]

Significantly, though these attitudes were expressed in 1968, they were based upon "retrospective" analyses, as if the event were finished and its lessons were to be identified so that the same mistakes would not be made in the future. Henry Kissinger's attitudes were those he brought with him when he assumed office on January 20, 1969. But the war continued, and virtually no new lessons were derived during the extension of hostilities and repetition of military miscalculations. Instead, the way to achieve an honorable peace—which by this time was synonymous with an honorable withdrawal, a positive disengagement—was assumed to be to negotiate from strength.

When Richard Nixon became President in 1969, the nation had 850,000 soldiers in Vietnam. Within months that number had increased to over one million. With the increase in personnel came a marked increase in weaponry, ships, planes, and helicopters. In 1970, under the guise of turning the war over to the South Vietnamese (a policy referred to as "Vietnamization"), the United States made the fateful decision to send troops into Cambodia. The President explained the decision to the American people by television: "If when the chips are down, the world's most powerful nation acts like a pitiful helpless giant, the forces of totalitarianism and anarchy will threaten free nations and free institutions throughout the world." He added that he would rather be a one-term President than preside over the nation's first defeat.[12]

The Cambodian incursion simply fanned the fires of discontent. Demonstrators poured out to protest all around the country. The first week in May, over one hundred thousand of them gathered in Washington to register their protest. Four college students were killed at Kent State University in confrontation with the National Guard, and college students everywhere went on strike. The riots in the community adjacent to the University of California at Santa Barbara resulted in the burning of a Bank of America building. Many campuses were forced to close for the summer break early.

The U.S. Senate terminated the Gulf of Tonkin Resolution of 1964, Senators Sherman Cooper of Kentucky and Frank Church of Idaho put forward a bill to cut off all funds for American military operations in Cambodia after June 30, and Senators Mark Hatfield and George McGovern proposal that all American forces be withdrawn from Vietnam by the end of 1971. The Hatfield-McGovern measure failed to pass in the Senate; the Cooper-Church proposal passed there, but failed in the House. Meanwhile, the President reiterated that American troops had been sent into Cambodia to attack the "nerve center" of the North Vietnamese operations. Later, Henry Kissinger explained the rationale for this action.

> There was no serious doubt that Hanoi's unopposed conquest of Cambodia would have been the last straw for South Vietnam. In the midst of a war, its chief ally was withdrawing forces at an accelerating rate and reducing its air support. Saigon was being asked to take the strain at the very moment Hanoi was increasing reinforcements greatly over the level of the preceding year. If Cambodia were to become a single armed camp at this point, catastrophe was inevitable. Saigon needed time to consolidate and improve its forces; the United States had to pose a credible threat for as long as possible; and Hanoi's offensive potential had to be weakened by slowing down its infiltration and destroying its supplies. It was a race between Vietnamization, American withdrawal, and Hanoi's offensives.[13]

Regardless of the strategic military value it may have had, the decision was enormously unpopular. The Nixon policies were not assisted by the trial of Lieutenant Calley in 1971 for the alleged murders of twenty-two Vietnamese citizens in the town of My Lai in 1968, nor by Daniel Ellsberg, who leaked Defense Department documents which illustrated that the nation's leaders had misled the American people. The President's reaction to these blows was to escalate and intensify American involvement in Vietnam even further, to the point that on May 8, 1972, the United States dropped thousands of tons of bombs on Haiphong Harbor, established a naval blockade of North Vietnam, and carried out continued extensive bombing raids over the territory.

Peace talks began on January 8, 1973, after Richard Nixon had been reelected and after heavy U.S. Christmas bombing raids over North Vietnam, but hostilities didn't cease until May 1, 1975. The Congress voted repeatedly to restrict American involvement, and the North Vietnamese troops marched virtually unopposed into Saigon, running their flag up the central flagpole and declaring to the world that Saigon was to be renamed Ho Chi Minh City. Richard Nixon had lost credibility with the American people, not as much for his Vietnam posture as through the Watergate scandal. It was left to President Ford to admit that United States military activity in Vietnam was finished.

Ford was called upon again and again to do just this. On February 6, 1975, certain distinguished members of the Congress filed a formal request under the auspices of a group called Members of Congress for Peace Through Law. Led by Senators Edward Brooke, Mark Hatfield, Frank Moss, and Edmund Muskie and by Representatives John Anderson, John Dellenback, Patsy Mink, and others, and supported by such prominent national leaders as Alan Cranston, George McGovern, Adlai Stevenson, Philip Hart, and Hubert Humphrey, the group wrote to the President:

> We remain resolute in our conviction, supported by the legislation passed in the 93rd Congress, that continuing American military and economic involvement in Indochina will not bring that unhappy region closer to a lasting peace. While continuing high levels of American assistance may perhaps prolong the life of the incumbent South Vietnamese and Cambodian governments, we can see no humanitarian or national interest that justifies the cost of this assistance to our country . . .

We believe the time is now at hand when our government must make a decision, too long postponed at a tragically high cost to both the people of Indochina and to our own citizens, as to how we will extricate ourselves from the situation in Southeast Asia once and for all.

We write to ask you and your most senior advisers to accept this expression of our views in a spirit of conciliation. We should get on with the important work ahead of us. Innovative leadership both from you and the Congress will be needed more than ever.

Accordingly, we are prepared for a serious, unemotional dialogue on the immediate problem of ending our involvement in Indochina responsibly and honorably. We are not prepared for it to continue indefinitely.[14]

The letter was signed by twelve senators and seventy members of the House of Representatives, among others.

On March 7 thirty-eight members of the House sent the President an even more forceful letter. Though the war had been winding down, the representatives objected to the recent infusion of American arms and money requested by the Ford administration.

We are writing to you, Mr. President, to let you know of our opposition to this aid request and to ask for your statesmanship in ending this tragedy . . .

For many of us, this war has been a constant backdrop, a permanent policy of our government, for most of our adult lives. We watched this war maim and kill our friends, and then maim and kill the trust of American people in their leaders. This war has created within our own government the necessity for deception and distortion. This war has not stood for our historic ideals, nor aided prosperity and happiness at home or in Southeast Asia.

The folly of it all has touched Americans personally and politically. As a new generation of politicians, we think we have been able to look at this disaster differently than many who were in responsibility over the last decade . . .

You and three other Presidents have tried with utmost sincerity to give to the countries of Southeast Asia the means to fight their internal wars. But history shows clearly that no outside power, however mighty, can regenerate another society or regime that does not have the inner will to maintain itself.

The request continues:

As the distinguished historian Barbara Tuchman wrote about the similar efforts of the United States to resurrect the Chiang Kai-shek regime: "In the end China went its own way as if the Americans have never come." In the same sense, Cambodia and South Vietnam will go their own ways; and at this point the American people have stated clearly that they have no interest in postponing this process. It is time for all of us to have the courage to face that reality at last.

The authors made it clear that they were neither blaming the President nor accusing others of being at fault.

Finally, Mr. President, we ask you to approach your decision and ours without recrimination. Our country will never heal the terrible wounds of this war if we try to blame each other for events that no single President or Congress could control . . .

Reminding the President that they shared awesome domestic responsibilities, the authors concluded:

We face our own war here at home against crippling economic developments, the crisis in energy and other public resources, and other serious problems. We will need to undertake strong action and strong debate under your leadership; it has never been more important that we act with good faith in this endeavor. But we cannot confront and resolve these crises while the United States continues involvement in Southeast Asia.[15]

To a significant degree, this was the growing consensus. Even those who had previously supported the war effort became disillusioned, somewhat chastened, and introspective.

The rupture of the collective morale had already occurred; the divisions within the country were deep. James R. Schlesinger, secretary of defense in both the Nixon and Ford administrations, was not alone in observing in 1975 that "the vitality of the nation's military establishment . . . its perceptions of itself, its precision of mission, flow from a sense of purpose deriving from [the] larger national unity and spirit." Against such necessary conditions, Schlesinger perceived that "vision and confidence have diminished" and "a vacuum of the spirit has appeared." For him, the transformation of the American temper raised a "grave question" as to "whether national unity, combined with freedom, still elicits a response sufficient that, in Lincoln's phrase, nations 'so conceived and so dedicated can long endure.'"[16]

The nation had done to itself what no external force could have accomplished: It was dispirited, lacking in confidence, unsure, trying to exist within a vacuum of context. It was an error in strategy to think that America could preside over comprehensive internal changes—redressing inequities among minority and disadvantaged people, finding an effective place among the developing and Third World nations, continuing to be successful in the exploration and use of outer space, managing natural resources judiciously, and so on—while claiming virtue for its involvement in a debilitating war whose intentions the American population could neither identify with nor fully adopt. It was just as foolish to believe that all of this could be achieved at once as it was to expect that a stable government could be imposed on South Vietnam without the clear request or firm mandate of the Vietnamese people. As the congressional letter enunciates, "No outside power, however mighty, can regenerate another society or regime that does not have the inner will to maintain itself."

The disillusion at home was expressed in a wide variety of ways, three of which we will examine in succeeding chapters: first, the form of response that has become prevalent among the veterans of combat; second, the turn to a more contemplative, some would say passive, orientation to human life; and, third, the desire to reestablish vibrant and vigorous American resolve through a reawakening of conservatism.

All agree that the Vietnam War spelled trauma for Americans. They might concede too that Vietnam's consequence was a malaise. But it is how various people accommodated themselves to the malaise that lent definition to competing chronicles of the American experience in the post-Vietnam years.

5. The Combatants

"Life, to be sure, is nothing much to lose. But young men think it is, and we were young."
— ALFRED EDWARD HOUSMAN

THE STORIES Vietnam veterans tell are virtually uniform in style, tone, direction, and content—intensely personal, eyewitness, reverse or revisionist conversion stories. Before they reach conclusions they break off, as if the chronicle doesn't go anywhere, as if it involves a plot that can find no resolution, as if the telling engages a sequence of deep emotional involvement that has been interrupted or is still trying desperately to find its way.

Characteristically, veterans place the macho portions of their story at the beginning. They make excited reference to athletic prowess or to an initial confidence in the ways, joys, and satisfactions of athletic competition. They talk about end-of-season tournaments, championships, trophies, newspaper articles, and accolades from their coaches, friends, family, and team fans. Success in competition seems to give confident formation to their world, and what is required to excel in athletics seems to be what is required to be successful in life. This is the temper of the stories one hears.

The links between the ways of competition and of warfare, or so the veterans supposed, are clear and direct. Competition is the stuff of life, and it transfers easily to the discipline of military involvement. It follows that one should approach devotion to one's country as an intensified and magnified expression of loyalty to the team. Fitting oneself for battle is like getting in shape for the championship; one has to be at one's best, prepared physically and mentally for the rigors that lie ahead. The soldier, like the athlete, knows that the decisive contest will prove to himself, in the presence of reliable witnesses, just who he is and how he looks relative to all others involved in the struggle. The prepared athlete relishes the competition, knowing that it will bring out the best in all who are involved, increasing their capacities and making them something that no other opportunity could encourage them to be. If they play well and seize the moment, they may become heroes, in their own eyes and in those of the faithful witnesses, who can be counted upon to express their adulation.

Obviously, there are both winners and losers in competition. When one is intent on winning, the thought of losing is repugnant. Losing is not merely second best; it is not-winning, and not winning means failure, which means that one's competitive impulses have been vanquished or have gone amiss. One can be a good sport about losing, but one never relinquishes the idea that winning is the purpose and competition the means of achievement.

A U.C.L.A. football coach once remarked that getting ready to play the team's cross-town rival, U.S.C., is like getting ready for war. He cited the pregame apprehensions and heightened emotions, the adrenalin flow, the intense sense of anticipation, the competitive fervor, and the recognition that one of the teams will win and the other lose, and the participants will be forced to live with that outcome for a long time. He told of the prayers before and after the game, when the players and coaches gather in their respective locker rooms for a moment of silence to request success in the upcoming fray and plead for the safety of all participants. It is this way each time, the coach related. Even if no one had planned it beforehand, the team would want to do it.

No one needs to explain the motivation in such situations. Being number one, whether in the city, the league, or the territory, is the purpose of competing. Who can imagine striving to become number two, unless, somehow, becoming number two is the best pathway toward being number one? Who can conceive of entering a competition that one really wishes to lose? If the team has entered the contest, it is to win, of course. That there is some alternative doesn't really enter one's mind. The rules of the game have been established so that justice will prevail, and if justice prevails, the right side should win – not easily, perhaps, but this will be the outcome for the deserving. So the contest will exhibit the laws of justice and propriety; it will provide support to our most cherished values, and demonstrate that right prevails over wrong, that good is victorious over evil, that the strongest can also be the most virtuous, and that a positive outcome is the reward for being prepared, fit, and appropriately resourceful.

These are some of the fundamental conceptions that became apparent when the American combatants in the Vietnam War returned home to tell of their experiences. The ones who went to Vietnam before 1967 tended to believe almost unquestionably in the propriety of U.S. interests and objectives. Even when confessing that they were not able fully to enunciate or provide a self-consistent rationale for it, they seemed to know why the United States found itself in Vietnam, and they believed the U.S. role to be in close keeping with the dictates of the national character. They also accepted as an indisputable fact that there was a job that needed to be done effectively, efficiently, decisively, and as swiftly as possible – the way most Americans like to work.

The goal was to repel Communist aggression, but the larger plot was the struggle of two antagonistic ways of life. Communism was alien to the way of life that had already made the United States great, and was challenging U.S. status as the model by which all of humankind, gradually but decisively, might come to enjoy greater individual and collective freedoms. The future course of international relationships, not to mention the long-range well-being of the planet, depended upon one side's ability to hold the other in check. The alternative – virtually inconceivable, given the confidence Americans shared in their sense of what human life should be – spelled the destruction of all that we prize most: our freedoms, privileges, and entitlements, our ability to communicate and worship as we please and to raise our children in whatever manner we desire.

Strangely, however, the alien form of life had gathered force. Its threats to the common good were spreading like a

disease. A line had to be drawn: *this far and no further*, as our
sacred Scriptures had sanctioned. What it meant to be an
American was to commit oneself to whatever was required to
insure that our fundamental freedoms would not be lost.
Therefore, the generation of young Americans called to do this
in Vietnam would certainly respond as generations of Americans had done in the past, during the First and Second World
Wars and, more recently, when the cancer of Communist
aggression was spreading into South Korea. We could be confident of this because it was through such situations that the
national character had been formed.

World War II left America with clear entitlement to the top
place on the ladder of international greatness, a position that
could be responsibly contested by only the Soviet Union. When
this was the case, who could imagine America becoming
number two? And who could conceive of an unanswered or
unacknowledged threat to the supremacy and superiority of
number one? If no response were offered, the rules of justice
would be threatened; the prospect that good would prevail over
evil would be challenged; the network of international law and
order would be menaced. Thus, it was appropriate to take up
arms, if need be, if only to make certain that the confident way
in which human life was ordered would be allowed to prevail
against resistance, defiance, and open challenge. To support the
American cause was to pledge oneself to the designs of the true,
the good, and even the most beautiful.

There was plenty of inspiration and provocation for such a
response in the early 1960s. American citizens were well aware
of the Soviet takeovers of Hungary, Czechoslovakia, Romania,
Poland, even Yugoslavia in the realignments following the
Second World War. They were acutely sensitive to the establishment of the Berlin Wall and the Iron Curtain, the presence
of Castro in Cuba, and the possibility that volatile nuclear
weapons a few miles offshore were trained on U.S. cities. They
had become acquainted with the unpredictable temperament
of Nikita Khrushchev, the bellicose Soviet leader, who had boor-
ishly banged his shoe on a table during the formal proceedings

of the United Nations. The struggle with Communist aggression had become specific and concrete near the Fifty-second
Parallel in Korea. Every postwar U.S. President had enunciated
the perils of being soft on communism, and their respective
secretaries of state had worked to implement these convictions
in the nation's foreign policy. None of these principles could be
attributed to partisan political interests; rather, the nation had
decided long ago, by implicit consensus, to defend its cherished
way of life against all threats.

Americans had gotten used to living this way over a long
period of time. The decision was implicit in our military battles;
it had also been responsible for the means by which our territory was tamed and settled. We had watched it in our films
about good guys versus bad guys, the clean-shaven ones in the
white hats versus the unshaved ones in the black hats. We had
grown accustomed to the Knotts Berry Farm virtues by which
the West was won. We knew that the story was over when the
hero rode out of town on his horse, leaving behind the successful resolution of conflict and a host of grateful and admiring
hearts.

When the image of the true American, the All-American,
wasn't John Wayne or Gary Cooper, it was Audie Murphy, Sergeant York, George Patton, Eisenhower, MacArthur. The con-
stitution of those we watched on the screen was the same as of
those on the athletic or battle fields. In all such situations, competition offered the conditions by which one could break
through the barriers to enter the world of unusual accomplishment. It enabled one to transcend the particularities and peculi-
arities of home, family, place of origin, individual endowment,
and to gain larger fame, recognition, and quite possibly fortune.

Many of the impulses sanctioned by the religious faith of
the land supported the same tendencies. Indeed, it would be
impossible to describe the dynamics of the Judeo-Christian
tradition without involving battle and warfare. The God of the
Old Testament is a deity who leads his people forth in battle, to
whom they can properly look for assistance in subduing the
power of their enemies. Christians sing "Onward, Christian

soldiers, marching as to war"; the primary hymn of the Protestant Reformation is Martin Luther's "A Mighty Fortress Is Our God," which contains such lines as "He breaks the cruel oppressor's rod and wins salvation glorious," and "holds the field victorious." The hymn sung most frequently in America at the time of the Civil War was Julia Ward Howe's "Battle Hymn of the Republic," in which "the coming of the Lord" is associated with "the fateful lightning of his terrible swift sword" as "our God is marching on."

But these are merely surface examples of the strong interdependencies of religion and warfare. The ease with which the deity is worshiped as "lord of all," "he who is mighty in battle," bespeaks the same connotations. Liturgical services take place in the presence of a throne. In much of the medieval Christian tradition, *lord* is all but synonymous with *warrior king,* and the Crusades indistinguishably mixed religious fervor with military prowess. In more recent history, when fifty-two U.S. hostages were released from captivity in Iran, many Americans found it appropriate to give thanks to God for their deliverance from the hand of our adversary.

Members of the armed services chaplaincies are acutely aware of these connections. The padres pray for both the safety of the troops and their success in battle before they leave camp to enter the fray, and the troops gather around, as they did when Cardinal Spellman came from New York to South Vietnam to give his blessing. Sometimes such practices became confusing, as Michael Herr reflects in his book, *Dispatches:*

> Prayers in the Delta, prayers in the Highlands, prayers in the Marine bunkers of the "frontier" facing the DMZ, and for every prayer there was a counterprayer—it was hard to see who had the edge. In Da Lat the emperor's mother sprinkled rice in her hair so the birds could fly around her and feed while she said her morning prayers. In wood-paneled, air-conditioned chapels in Saigon, MAVC padres would fire one up to sweet muscular Jesus, blessing ammo dumps and 105's and officers' clubs. The best-armed patrols in history went out after services to feed

smoke to people whose priests could let themselves
burn down to consecrated ash on street corners. Deep
in the alleys you could hear small Buddhist chimes
ringing for peace, *hoa bien*; smell incense in the middle of the thickest Asian street funk; see groups of
ARVN with their families waiting for transport hud-
dled around a burning prayer strip. Sermonettes came
over Armed Forces Radio every couple of hours. Once
I heard a chaplain from the 9th Division starting up,
"Oh Gawd, help us to learn to live with Thee in a more
dynamic way in these perilous times, that we may
better serve Thee in the struggle against Thine enemies . . ." Holy war, long-nose jihad like a face-off
between one god who would hold the coonskin to the
wall while we nailed it up, and another whose detach-
ment would see the blood run out of ten generations,
if that was how long it took for the wheel to go
around.[1]

Indeed, the Western predisposition to link warfare and
religion in this manner was at least partly responsible for the
perplexities many westerners experienced when confronting
the self-immolation of Buddhist monks before the fall of the
Diem regime in 1963. Frances FitzGerald describes this situation in her prizewinning book, *Fire in the Lake:*

Just before the fall of the Diem regime in 1963, the
American journalists in Vietnam wrote long and
somewhat puzzling analyses of the Buddhist demonstrations in which they attempted to explain how
much the rebellion against Diem owed to "purely religious" motives, how much to "purely political" ones.
Like most Westerners these journalists were so
entrenched in the Western notion of the division of
church and state that they could not imagine the Vietnamese might not make the distinction. But until the
arrival of the European missionaries there was never
such a thing as a church in Vietnam. Shaped by a
millennium of Chinese rule and another of independence within the framework of Southeast Asia, the
"Vietnamese religion" was a blend of Confucianism,
Taoism, and Buddhism sunken into the background of
animism. More than a "religion" in any Western sense,
it was the authority for, and the confirmation of, an

entire way of life – an agriculture, a social structure, a political system.[2]

While westerners may have missed the synthetic integration of Vietnamese social and cultural life, they did find it appropriate to call upon their own deity for assistance against the enemy. Such a deity can be relied upon to aid the victims of unjustified aggression, but not the aggressor. It is therefore important to be able to prove that "the other side started it," and that one is merely defending oneself against unwarranted intervention. Americans could religiously sanction the United States' entrance into World War II because the Germans had been seizing European land and the Japanese had bombed Pearl Harbor, but the story would have been vastly different had the action come from the United States. Similarly, the United States sought public sympathy for its cause in Vietnam because it sided with those who had been victimized by aggression, the South Vietnamese. Ho Chi Minh was the agent of aggression, and the United States was responding to the call to quell him so that evil would not be allowed to prosper.

This may help explain how the United States combatants justified to themselves their roles in the Vietnam War. The opportunity for heroism was there, because unwarranted aggression had been loosed. The contest between the forces of good and evil was implicit, too, because blatant aggression involves illegal seizure of power and of territory belonging to others. The cause seemed to be just, because it carried the blessings of the nation's collective sense of purpose, in the form – at least at first – of the clergy's willingness to invoke benediction.

Before the hostilities could cease, however, many of the clergy found themselves taking up the banner of the protestors – an action that left many of the combatants deeply confused and seriously disoriented. They sensed that their actions no longer had the support of the nation's collective purpose, and perhaps that the same purpose was no longer well grounded. Thus, the opportunity for heroic action was transposed into its opposite: The warriors came home not as victors, as they had expected, but as victims. Even when their gallantry was the highest of which human beings are capable, they returned as losers, because circumstances had positioned them on ignominy's side. The recompense they sought could only be gained if they were to move to a sanctioned position – that is, to identification with the war protestors, who acknowledged that the collective sense of purpose had not held and that the combat did not deserve either patriotic or religious legitimization.

The autobiographical literature through which the story of the war in Vietnam is being told is replete with testimony to the conflicted resolve, anguish, and ambivalence the combatants experienced. One of the most graphic accounts is that provided by Philip Caputo in *A Rumor of War*, in which the initial invitation to heroic action is issued by President John F. Kennedy during his Inaugural Address, with the words "Ask not what your country can do for you; ask what you can do for your country." Caputo writes:

> This is what I wanted, to find in a commonplace world a chance to live heroically. Having known nothing but security, comfort, and peace, I hungered for danger, challenges, and violence.
>
> I had no clear idea of how to fulfill this peculiar ambition until the day a Marine recruiting team set up a stand in the student union at Loyola University. They were on a talent hunt for officer material and displayed a poster of a trim lieutenant who had one of those athletic, slightly cruel-looking faces considered handsome in the military. He looked like a cross between an All-American halfback and a Nazi tank commander. Clear and resolute, his blue eyes seemed to stare at me in challenge. JOIN THE MARINES, read the slogan above his white cap. BE A LEADER OF MEN . . .
>
> I rummaged through the propaganda material, picking out one pamphlet whose cover listed every battle the Marines had fought, from Trenton to Inchon. Reading down that list, I had one of those rare flashes of insight: the heroic experience I sought was war; war, the ultimate adventure; war, the ordinary man's

most convenient means of escaping from the ordinary.
The country was at peace then, but the early sixties
were years of almost constant tension and crisis; if a
conflict did break out, the Marines would be certain
to fight in it and I could be there with them. Actually
there. Not watching it on a movie or TV screen, not
reading about it in a book but *there*, living out a
fantasy.

Then comes some cinematic imagery:

Already I saw myself charging up some distant
beachhead, like John Wayne in *Sands of Iwo Jima*, then
coming home a suntanned warrior with medals on my
chest. The recruiters started giving me the usual sales
pitch, but I hardly needed to be persuaded. I decided
to enlist.

At the end of the three-year enlistment period, after
Caputo had been in the midst of the Vietnam War, he felt
differently.

I came home from the war with the curious feeling
that I had grown older than my father, who was then
fifty-one. It was as if a lifetime of experience had been
compressed into a year and a half. A man saw the
heights and depths of human behavior in Vietnam, all
manner of violence and horrors so grotesque that they
evoked more fascination than disgust. Once I had
seen pigs eating napalm-charred corpses—a memo-
rable sight, pigs eating roast people.

His aspirations had been altered, too.

I was left with none of the optimism and ambition a
young American is supposed to have, only a desire to
catch up on sixteen months of missed sleep and an old
man's conviction that the future would hold no further
surprises, good or bad.
I hoped there would be no more surprises. I had
survived enough ambushes and doubted my capacity
to endure many more physical and emotional shocks.
I had all the symptoms of *combat veteranitis*: an inability to concentrate, a childlike fear of darkness, a
tendency to tire easily, chronic nightmares, an intoler-
ance of loud noises—especially doors slamming and

cars backfiring – and alternating moods of depression and rage that came over me for no apparent reason. Recovery has been less than total.

Summing it up, Caputo writes;

> Beyond adding a few more corpses to the weekly body count, none of the encounters achieved anything; none will ever appear in military histories or be studied by cadets at West Point. Still, they changed us and taught us, the men who fought in them; in those obscure skirmishes we learned the old lessons about fear, cowardice, courage, suffering, cruelty, and comradeship. Most of all, we learned about death at an age when it is common to think of oneself as immortal. Everyone loses that illusion eventually, but in civilian life it is lost in installments over the years. We lost it all at once and, in the span of months, passed from boyhood through manhood to a premature middle age. The knowledge of death, of the implacable limits placed on man's existence, severed us from our youth as irrevocably as a surgeon's scissors had once severed us from the womb. And yet, few of us were past twenty-five. We left Vietnam peculiar creatures, with young shoulders that bore rather old heads.[3]

The "old-man" theme Caputo enunciates is prominent in the combat literature. Gloria Emerson, for example, writes of Albert Lee Reynolds, who was employed for two years as an engineer in Bangkok, from which he was frequently sent into Vietnam. Experiencing the horror of the war, Reynolds launched his own anti-Patton campaign against

> those in the military who called for war and needed the battle, eyes and mouths fierce with pleasure when they plunged into it, wanting the breaking and the bleeding and the moans, dragging with them into the darkness soldiers who were only boys and could not run away from such cruel and powerful new fathers.[4]

When Reynolds was called upon to speak on "The Vietnam War: Consciousness and Conscience" to a meeting of the American Orthopsychiatric Association in New York, he began:

I was a young man when we – my wife and I – set
out to explore the world . . . the first overseas job was
in Africa – that was the beginning – in and out of air-
ports, strange ports in countries I had read about as a
boy in geography class in Oklahoma. My wife was
twenty-two and I was twenty-nine when it all began.
When it was over, five years later, my wife was
twenty-seven and I was an old man.

In those days they were being slaughtered like
animals – in droves – fresh from the high school study
halls and the after-school football practice and from
working on their old cars. Those were the days of
Hamburger Hill. I wonder – I always will – what the
real motivation was for the officers who made them
run up Hamburger Hill to die. Was their motivation a
mistaken belief that they were helping America? Or
were they thinking about their next promotion and
their combat proficiency report and their career
records back in the Pentagon?

Emerson reports that as Reynolds proceeded, "his voice was not
even. People were silent, as if he were pulling them into a place
they had not been and did not want to go." He continued: "Even
animals – even animals – protect their young."[5]

Lee Childress was a sergeant in the 206th Assault
Helicopter Company, serving in Vietnam from June 1967 to
May 1968. He records how it felt to watch an American soldier
shoot and kill an old Vietnamese woman after catching her
trying to steal his spearmint gum.

He shot her point-blank through the chest and
killed her. Even now, every time I see spearmint gum
it blows me right out of the fucking saddle, man . . .
for a fucking piece of gum. We got in more trouble for
killing water buffalo than we did for killing people.
That was something I could never adjust to.

Childress confesses that the imagery has stayed with him.

Today I go down the street and I see things in a way
that nobody else sees them. I look at my own kid and
it scares me. 'Cause it's a baby, and babies are alive
and they're beautiful and they're perfect, and they've
got arms and legs and feet and toes, and their mind is

like an empty plate that hasn't had all these things happen to it. And I think, "If you ever saw what I've seen. If you'd spent the time that I spend every fucking day of my life, going over and over again the *why?* and the *why?* and I always know there's no answer." There's no answer anywhere. And that really scares me sometimes.[6]

Childress's story is corroborated by thousands of other veterans who experienced the assumption that the Vietnamese were subhuman or nameless creatures. David Ross, who was a medic with the 1st Infantry Division in Vietnam from December 1965 to July 1967, described the skewed perceptions this way:

When Americans are talking about Vietnamese or people in India or somewhere similar, it's not like we're looking at them like they're our next-door neighbors. If someone came to our neighborhood and burned all of our houses and most of our possessions and put us in flying saucers which we'd never seen before and zipped us across the universe, setting us down somewhere in tent city in the middle of a sandbox with wire all around us, I guess we might not be too excited about it. Most of us were never able to see the Vietnamese as real people . . .

I remember President Johnson in one of the psy-op [psychological warfare] flicks we saw saying that the communists weren't like us — they didn't have feelings. But I always remembered that old woman or remembered after a B-52 strike going into this area where there was a little girl with her leg . . . traumatic amputation . . . and . . . still alive. Her mother dead. The whole place turned upside down, a few people still screaming, some people wandering around with the look of the dead, a totally shocked daze.

The scene caused Ross to ponder:

I wondered how people would feel in Pittsburgh if the Vietnamese came over in B-52s and bombed them . . . I'm trying to imagine a bunch of steelworkers after their wives, children, fiancées, parents, grandparents, have been blown up or are running around screaming in agony and some Vietnamese pilot comes swooping

down in a parachute. I don't imagine they'd give him a
very friendly reception.[7]

Fred Downs, leader of an infantry squad, had a similar
reaction to the plundering of the Vietnamese countryside:

> They sent me in there. I stomped across people's
> rice paddies. I didn't know what I was. I couldn't
> speak their language. My concern was to keep my
> men alive. And if there were any people in the village,
> I couldn't think of them as being anything other than
> the enemy. And so I was a soldier, doing what soldiers
> do, which is to piss people off in the country we've
> entered.
> You know, I think about this a lot. On my farm in
> Indiana, if I had a squad of Vietnamese come through
> and stomp through my garden the way I did, go
> through my house the way I went through their
> houses, and search, and kill all the chickens and cows,
> you know, this wouldn't do anything to win my heart
> and mind. However, I was a young man then. I hadn't
> been trained to think. I had been trained to kill. And
> that's what I did. I became very good at it. But luckily
> I survived, and now am able to think back on what I
> did.[8]

The confusion, misconceptions, and inaccurate preconcep-
tions were abundant. Ross remembers the way he was
instructed to think of Ho Chi Minh:

> The first thing that really hit me was just after we
> arrived in Vietnam, during our initial reception
> period. We were told not to bad-mouth Ho Chi Minh,
> since the Vietnamese mistakenly thought he was the
> George Washington of their country because he had
> thrown out the French; but they didn't understand
> that he was a communist and would bring them to a
> sticky end.[9]

Murray Fromsen, television correspondent for CBS News
during the war years in Vietnam, believes the misrepresentations were sustained because Americans were not yet accustomed to viewing Asians as human, at least not human in the
same way that Americans understand themselves to be.

Fromsen refers to "the fear of the yellow horde," and recalls an incident during the Korean War that illustrates the attitude.

> It was up around the 38th Parallel, and we were in a
> chow line. There was a group of hungry Koreans,
> civilians, outside the barbed wire with their hands
> out, asking for food. They were starving. And they
> yelled "Chop-chop, chop-chop." We had plenty of
> food. But our officers told us to throw the food away.
> We couldn't afford to have the Koreans on our back,
> following us around. It was a security problem. I
> remember going up to the captain at the time and
> saying, "What if these people had been Belgian, or
> Italian, or white?"

Fromsen believes that the same attitude was present in the Vietnam situation, and offers the following as illustration:

> I was in Cambodia, and I remember a discussion I
> had at the American Embassy about three weeks
> before Phnom Penh fell. It was with a senior official
> of the Embassy who has since died. He tried to
> explain that the U.S. role in Cambodia was designed
> to head off a blood bath by the Khmer Rouge. I had
> been there for some time, and had been in Cambodia
> in the fifties when it was a rather tranquil country. I
> said, "Well, if we're heading off a blood bath by the
> Khmer Rouge, what is it we are doing now with our
> continued support of this government, by continuing
> to supply it with arms, weapons, with the killings and
> woundings, the orphans, widows, seven hundred
> thousand people, perhaps, being affected by the war?"
> His response was, "We think our people are more
> moral than theirs. Our people believe in the principles
> of Erasmus."
> Dumbfounded I said, "What has Erasmus got to do
> with Cambodia?"[10]

Fromsen's observations are corroborated by the testimony of Shad Meshad, a psychology officer in Vietnam. For Meshad it was a shock to confront Asia and Asians:

> I was from the southeastern part of the United
> States, and spent my entire life there. I knew nothing
> about the northeast or even about the southwest. And,
> for sure, I didn't know a thing about Asia.

So it was like an overnight event. The first thing I knew I was in Asian culture. And the biggest, most traumatic thing that I ever had to deal with was the opposite culture – the completely different way of life that Asia presented to me.

Sure it was war. Sure it was guns. Sure it was blood, sweat and tears. But I knew nothing about Asians. The only thing I did know about them were the names we gave them, both four-letter words, "gook" and "dink." And our attitude was that the only good dink is a dead dink. This was my introduction to the culture of Asia.

Meshad elaborates:

I went over there, so I was told, to protect Asians from communism. But I went as a health-care person. And when I arrived it was like, is this it?

Well, without saying any more, I think that much of the guilt the Vietnam veteran feels is due to the fact that he went in, like I did, and was used and manipulated. He had to abuse the culture to stay alive. Since coming back, he has mourned the fact that he never even understood. And the moment he did begin to understand, he perceived that the American involvement was wrong.

No, we didn't understand the culture. We thought, "Well, if it's communist, we have the obligation to fight it." It didn't matter that we didn't understand the language they spoke, their history, the situation that belonged to them. No, we just went in there like superstars. We're red, white and blue! We're John Wayne! We do it![11]

As Meshad's testimony illustrates, the misrepresentations, misconceptions, and skewed anticipations created profound disillusionment. Karl Phaler, who advised the Vietnamese navy for a year beginning in December 1966, relates the impression that affected him most:

I was talking about American steel dismembering Vietnamese children for no apparent purpose. I was horribly distressed that having dismembered the children, we couldn't at least . . . The responsibility, damnit. Remember I said I was responsible? I wanted somebody else to help. We ought to be responsible. It wasn't enough to stop a war. I couldn't go back to Washington and tell Lyndon, "Look, you're hearing lies filtered and purified fifteen times. Everything you're hearing about the war is crap. Stop it." I wasn't going to stop the war. What needed to be done was some after-services. There ought to have been someone helping to order the carnage around a little bit. If we're going to inflict so much misery, I felt at least we had a moral obligation, which is the most compelling kind I know, to do something to alleviate the misery that we'd inflicted. Like care for broken children, for starters.[12]

Frequently the disillusionment set in after the combatants returned home to an ambivalent reception. Many veterans cite the alienating experience of arriving at Travis Air Force Base near Sacramento, often wounded and sometimes just hours away from the battlefield in Vietnam, to meet the jeers, taunts, tomatoes, and spittle of the antiwar protestors lining their pathway. For others the disorientation was cumulative; days and weeks and months of reflection on the war forced them to experience the disillusionment keenly.

Downs, a wounded veteran who won four Purple Hearts, the Bronze Star for Valor, and the Silver Star, recalls the welcome he received:

In the fall of 1968, as I stopped at a traffic light on my walk to class across the campus of the University of Denver, a man stepped up to me and said, "Hi."
Without waiting for my reply to his greeting, he pointed to the hook sticking out of my left sleeve. "Get that in Vietnam?"
I said, "Yeah, up near Tam Ky in I Corps."
"Serves you right."
As the man walked away, I stood rooted, too confused with hurt, shame, and anger to react.[13]

Downs says he was stunned that anyone could say anything so cruel.

He also tells of an event that happened just a few months later:

I went to downtown Denver to have my photograph taken with me in my uniform. The photographer and owner of the shop had been in World War II, and had been in business in Denver for many years. He asked me a lot of questions. I didn't want to talk about Vietnam. I just wanted to have my picture taken for my family back home in Indiana. But he kept prying, asking questions, and suddenly became very angry with me because he accused me of pushing people out of helicopters, torturing prisoners, all sorts of things that I had never done. All I did was go to war, come back from war, and do what I was told. But when I left the photographer, and went back home, in the silence of my home, I broke down and cried, because I didn't understand it. It was completely beyond me.

Downs also remembers being at a party in 1969, when someone was excited about a moon landing. Downs was asked if he would take a gun to the moon if he had the chance to go. He said, "What kind of question is that? Why would you ask me this?" And his interrogator responded, "Well, since you were in Vietnam, you would want a gun with you, wouldn't you, so you could kill anyone who disagreed with you?"

Downs pleads that he was only an infantry soldier who went to war because he was asked to do so by the country for which he fought. He explains:

I had had it hammered in me from my first awareness that fighting for your country is a good thing. In any other war, my fellow soldiers and I would have returned home to our country's accolades. Then we would have picked up our lives and gone on with our futures, secure in the knowledge that we had done right. But Vietnam was different . . .
No one could explain exactly why we were there, but they kept asking the soldier why he was there in the hope that the soldier had the answer. He didn't, of course, certainly no more than did Congress or the executive branch. But unfortunately for the soldier, a historical paradox was occurring in that Americans began to hate war, and Americans didn't know how to separate the strong feelings they had against Vietnam

and war and the soldiers who were sent. There was no common denominator of patriotism. The Nam soldier got caught in the crossfire. If war is wrong, and that war in particular was wrong, the soldier was wrong for fighting it.[14]

William Jayne, a rifleman in a Marine company, who was wounded near Khe Sanh in 1968, put it this way:

We went to Vietnam as frightened lonely young men. We came back, alone again, as immigrants to a new world. For the culture we had known dissolved while we were in Vietnam, and the culture of combat we lived in so intensely for a year made us aliens when we returned.[15]

A similar disillusionment was experienced by those who felt compelled to resist the draft, one of whom, Eddie Correia, expressed himself on the subject as follows:

Vietnam, at least for three or four years, hovered over my life and the lives of those around me. It was the source of scores of discussions about the folly of our involvement and the focus of shared views about how drastically wrong political leaders could be. It was, I believe, the strongest force driving young people to distrust their leaders and to destroy what they felt was worst about American life.[16]

Yet, as James Fallows testifies, resisting the draft did not exempt an individual from feelings of shame and guilt:

Among those who went to war, there is a residual resentment, the natural result of a cool look at who ended up paying what price. On the part of those who were spared, there is a residual guilt, often so deeply buried that it surfaces only in unnaturally vehement denials that there is anything to feel guilty about.

In a land of supposed opportunity, the comfortable hate to see the poor. Beneath all the explanations about self-help and just desserts, there remains the vein of empathy and guilt. Among the bright people of my generation, those who have made a cult of their high-mindedness, the sight of legless veterans and the memories of the Navy Yard must also touch that vein. They remind us that there was little character in the choices we made.[17]

The disillusionment and ambivalence was thorough, and was experienced by people on every side of the issue. Because of the vivid television portrayals of the war, those at home shared the emotions of the direct participants. Peter Tauber catches this mood in his novel. *The Last Best Hope:*

> All over, a dreary mood had settled in. No lever could be found to move the world. The war had become, for many at home, the source of fruitless contention; for others, a new idiom of entertainment: in the evenings they could turn a dial and "watch the war." To some it existed solely because it was on every channel. If not palpable, it was nonetheless undeniable. People had begun to chant that "things were in the saddle," and to feel that their lives were at the mercy of forces, great or infinitesimal, beyond their control: overwhelming vectors, insuperable momentum, genetic and historical.

Tauber reported that what was happening both in Vietnam and throughout the nation was "contrary to American Faith."

> To many it was hard to believe. And so it was not believed. It was not so much a heroic refusal as it was romantic. For belief itself was the greatest agony. What was held as true was disappointing; what was hoped for seemed impossible. Cherished values trembled. Dear faiths brought the most painful and paradoxical returns: the best intentions in the world murdered and maimed and ruined.[18]

Frequently the outcome was expressed in terms of athletic competition. Bruce Lawlor, who was employed by the CIA in Vietnam from November 1971 to December 1973, describes it this way:

> I think the North Vietnamese played us better than we know. They just totally out-psyched us. We lost the war because of will, not military power . . . I think initially they probably didn't recognize what they were on to . . . but our reaction in the United States was so overwhelming—I mean, it toppled the President—that all of a sudden it became clear to them that they could make the Americans beat themselves.[19]

David Ross put the matter in similar terms:

> . . . the United States had practically committed itself
> to the fact that it wasn't going to win and it was just
> going to be a question of which President would be
> unlucky enough to be in power when the thing was
> lost. It was like a dirty football and it just got passed
> along. Ford seemed to be the guy they agreed to dump
> it on. It had fallen apart and he wasn't elected, and for
> better or worse, the timing all came together at that
> point.[20]

James Bombard, a rifle platoon leader, agrees:

> I think we lost a lot more in Vietnam than the
> troops we lost. We really didn't lose too many battles.
> When we met the enemy we usually won. What did
> we win? We lost more than we won, especially the
> aftermath of the war. Having served in Vietnam,
> having served in the infantry, having been wounded,
> feeling the bullet rip into your flesh, the shrapnel tear
> the flesh from your bones and the blood run down
> your leg, and feeling like you're gonna piss in your
> pants and it's the blood running down your leg. To put
> your hand on your chest and to come away with your
> hand red with your own blood, and to feel it running
> out of your eyes and out of your mouth, and seeing it
> spurt out of your guys, realizing you were dying . . .[21]

Gloria Emerson tells of a sixty-two-year-old Baptist minister who would like to see a monument erected in Washington,
dedicated to Vietnam veterans and inscribed: "When you send
us to war, make sure you give us everything we need to win. Or
don't send us." The minister's attitude is that "the Congress and
the President didn't have the will to win the war or the guts to
call it off. It was all for nothing."[22] Emerson also provides this
statement by a veteran:

> Look at me, yes, look at me. There is no way I'll buy
> the American dream again. I've seen what we've done
> to people. I see what we do to people in prisons, I've
> seen it in Vietnam. I've seen it in the civil-rights move-
> ment. I mean you're never going to sell me that shit
> again. That's all there is to it. There were a lot of
> people clubbed in Chicago who said that the system is

all screwed up and who are now driving Cadillacs and working as IBM salesmen. But they had experience, they got some foresight into the system. That's never going to be purged; it has a carry-over that is never going to be taken away from them.[23]

William Mahedy of San Diego, a chaplain in the war and subsequently a counselor for the Veterans Administration, tells of a former combatant who expressed his disillusion this way: "I believed in Jesus Christ and John Wayne before I went to Vietnam. After Vietnam, both went down the tubes." Mahedy summarizes from his years of experience listening and talking with combatants:

> What is bothering a lot of them is a deep-seated moral and religious malaise. Even those who have slipped back into the American mainstream seem to experience a vague feeling of unease, suffering in varying degrees from spiritual debilitation . . .
> Characteristics are similar to those found in the clinical syndrome. The sense of guilt, the feeling of having been victimized or scapegoated by the government, resistance to moral and spiritual authorities, cynicism toward institutions and authorities formerly believed and trusted . . . a kind of spiritual numbness. The reservoir of moral resources has run dry. There is even alienation from one's feelings.[24]

When social analysts try to make sense of feelings like this, they talk about dysfunctional, nonadaptive traits or conditions. They try to explain how social integration and cultural coherence have become broken and disjointed, but it is only when the organism is sound and functioning well that definitions come easily and categories of interpretation fall into place relatively quickly. When anthropologist Clifford Geertz writes about the "cultural system," citing the influence of "symbols," "long-lasting moods and motivations," "conceptions of a general order of existence," and the like, he is referring to cultures that are intact.[25] We can understand motivation when we share an explicit purpose, when we understand the social order to be an accurate reflection of fundamental reality – that is, when the organism is integral and whole. But in Vietnam the consensus came apart; the sense of shared purpose was decimated, the basis of motivation became unclear, and conceptions of a general order of existence were unsure. As Morris Dickstein put it, the myth of America was broken. When this occurred, no one had any longer a firm hold on the American dream.

The response to this chaotic state assumed a variety of forms. Understandably, many become predominantly concerned about their own welfare and survival, reasoning that if reality really does consist of an almost random collection of bit parts – atoms whirling about in space – it is important to protect oneself against being hit and the likelihood of being destroyed. William Mahedy reports that

> in Vietnam, there seemed to be neither past nor future, only the very meaningless present. One could die in a combat assault upon a useless piece of ground for which men had died the month before and would die again next month. People were killed, bodies broken, spirit seared and scarred for what seemed to be totally senseless goals.
> The task in Vietnam was to survive until the freedom bird returned one to the world. The GIs themselves described their Vietnam experience in a perfect one-liner: "It don't mean nothin'."[26]

Michael Herr confirms that in the face of "the inversion of the expected order," "everyone was just trying to get through it, existential crunch, no atheists in foxholes like you wouldn't believe." He elaborates on how religious faith functions in a situation like this:

> Even bitter refracted faith was better than none at all, like the black Marine I'd heard about during heavy shelling at Con Thien who said, "Don't worry, baby, God'll think of something."
> Flip religion, it was so far out, you couldn't blame anybody for believing anything. Guys dressed up in Batman fetishes, I saw a whole squad like that, it gave them a kind of dumb esprit. Guys stuck the aces of spades in their helmet bands, they picked relics off of an enemy they'd killed, a little transfer of power; they carried around five-pound Bibles from home, crosses,

> St. Christophers, mezuzahs, locks of hair, girlfriends'
> underwear, snaps of their families, their wives, their
> dogs, their cows, their cars, pictures of John Kennedy,
> Lyndon Johnson, Martin Luther King, Huey Newton,
> the Pope, Che Guèvara, the Beatles, Jimi Hendrix,
> wiggier than cargo cultists. One man was carrying an
> oatmeal cookie through his tour, wrapped up in foil
> and plastic and three pair of socks. He took a lot of
> shit about it ("When you go to sleep we're gonna eat
> your fucking cookie"), but his wife had baked it and
> mailed it to him, he wasn't kidding.[27]

In the face of "the inversion of the expected order," the tech-
nique is to take self-protective measures to ensure one's
survival.

There was also the route of withdrawal. Lawrence Baskir
and William Strauss have estimated that nearly nine million
American men eligible for the draft managed to get deferred or
exempted. One hundred thousand eligible draftees deserted,
and more than two hundred thousand were officially charged
with violating the draft laws, though only three thousand actually went to jail. The same authors report that fifteen million
men of draft age completely avoided even one day of military
service; among those serving in Vietnam, only twenty-four
soldiers were convicted of deserting under fire. Such figures
show that "the Vietnam generation" included approximately
twenty-seven million draft-age men. Baskir and Strauss
contend that "until Americans evaluate the conduct of these
men [deserters and draft resisters] in the context of the entire
generation's response to the war, there can never be any real
understanding of the tragedy of Vietnam."[28]

The actions of draft evaders were supported by a 1971
Harris survey which found that a majority of American citizens
believed that those who agreed to serve in Vietnam were
"suckers, having to risk their lives in the wrong war, in the
wrong place, at the wrong time."[29] Clearly the antiwar movement was one of the prominent ways through which one could
exercise withdrawal.

The same interpretation should be applied to President Lyndon Johnson's action on March 31, 1968, when he announced to a stunned nation via television that he would not run for a second term as President. His intention undoubtedly was to withdraw so that whatever efforts he could still give to the cause of peace could not be interpreted as being motivated by self-gain, but his action was withdrawal nonetheless.

The process of "Vietnamization" championed by President Nixon, particularly from 1970 to the end of his office as commander-in-chief, also qualifies as a form of departure and disengagement. In *The Best and the Brightest*, David Halberstam describes the Nixon policy this way:

> . . . it would be Vietnamization, we would pull back American troops, probably to 250,000 by 1970, and perhaps to as few as 75,000 by 1972. There would be fewer and fewer Americans on the ground.

Judging the President's intention, Halberstam continues:

> So, he was dealing with war without really coming to terms with it; it was the compromise of a by now embattled President who knew he had to get American troops out but who still believed in their essential mission. So now he sought peace with honor. "What President Nixon means by peace," wrote Don Oberdorfer in the Washington *Post*, "is what other people mean by victory."[30]

"Vietnamization" came as close to withdrawal as political and cultural realities would allow.

Another response to the chaos of Vietnam was the surrealistic route, in which the inversion of the expected order is understood to be normative or expected. Here a person comes to accept the incongruous rules and seeming unnatural juxtapositions; access to reliable order is achieved through mental free associations, and the prevailing sense of life is derived from the world of the unconscious and the imaginary, as expressed in dreams and fantasies. For example, in the film *Apocalypse Now* one of the combatants in the midst of battle spots some inviting ocean waves and decides to go surfing.

Michael Herr, whose book *Dispatches* informed *Apocalypse Now*, also positions himself surrealistically:

> You'd stand nailed there in your tracks sometimes, no bearings and none in sight, thinking, *Where the fuck am I?*, fallen into some unnatural East-West interface, a California corridor cut and bought and burned deep into Asia and once we'd done it we couldn't remember what for. It was axiomatic that it was about ideological space, we were there to bring them the choice, bringing it to them like Sherman bringing the Jubilee through Georgia, clean through it, wall to wall with pacified indigenous and scorched earth.[31]

This was one of the pathways of release, but it created the possibility that the locus of the war would be almost completely transferred from Asian soil to American self-consciousness; then, once this had occurred, all collective psychological dysfunctions would be projected onto the battlefield. In this interpretation, the war in Vietnam was a projection of the deep sickness and ambivalence within the American soul. Americans were at war with themselves; the skirmishes with the Vietcong were secondary to the battles within our own collective unconsciousness.

Jan Barry, a radio technician involved in Vietnam early in 1962 and 1963, writes that it didn't take him very long to recognize that

> *we* were the war. If we wanted to go out and chase people around and shoot at them and get them to shoot back at us, we had a war going on. If we didn't do that, they left us alone. After a while it became clear that there was a pattern here. Our people, including Special Forces, used to stop at four-thirty and have a happy hour and get drunk. There was no war after four-thirty. On Saturday, no war. On Sundays, no war. On holidays, no war. That's right, a nine-to-five war. [32]

Given the fact that we could instigate war when we felt like it, even though we called our opponent the aggressor, the most crucial factors were motivation, moral resolve, and collective will. When the overarching meaning or scheme was no longer resonant and thus no longer legitimate, we had a clear sign that coherence was not intact: The enemy was internalized.

In the battles of the 1960s and 1970s, the external enemy seemed not to suffice. Mario Savio directed his vengeance not against the people of Vietnam, or the Soviet Union, or even communism, but against those in power within his own country. Joseph McCarthy had pointed his accusations against people outside, to be sure, but he had also contended that the enemy had invaded internally to threaten our basic security and was to be found where we least expected it. The Vietnam War protestors were most upset about the policies of the leadership of their own nation; for them, too, the primary adversary lurked internally. The combatants who fought bravely, like Phil Caputo, returned home to join the antiwar movement and direct their energies against those in charge of the government. Before the end of the 1960s, the antigovernment cause was taken up by those who perceived no other pathway toward election to the primary positions within government. To acknowledge the reality of the inversion of the expected order had become a precondition to the assumption of power.

In summary, the Vietnam War "games" were played with no clear sense of the rules. There were no winners, only losers, because the conception of winning had become thoroughly complex through the shattering of the expected order. Nevertheless, one of the outcomes of competitive involvement was sustained: The decisive contest did indeed demonstrate to all of us, in the presence of reliable witnesses, just who we were and how we looked relative to all others involved in the struggle.

6. West Meets East

*"But the great epics must mean something, not by
didactic pedagogy, propaganda, or edification, but by
their action, a murky metaphysical historical
significance, a sober intuition into the character of a
nation."*

— ROBERT LOWELL

WHEN HISTORIES OF the Vietnam War are written decades
from now, much will be made of the ways in which it contrib-
uted positively to cross-cultural understanding. This may seem
like a strange suggestion, but there is basis for it in responses
that have been present from the first. The general thesis is that
the impact of the war assisted westerners, Americans in particular, in appreciating the sense of life fundamental to portions
of Asian religions.[1]

This appreciation began with Hiroshima and the acute
awareness that every aspect of human life had been altered by
the dawning of the nuclear age. Before the nuclear capability
was developed, mankind could keep warfare within manage-
able bounds; its catastrophes were always of finite proportions.
But the explosions in Japan changed the meaning of war and, as
Robert Lifton has pointed out, altered perceptions of life.

Lifton noted in *Death in Life: Survivors of Hiroshima* and in
Boundaries that the fundamental sets of patterns by which
human life was approached and mediated had undergone radical change. Heretofore, life had been the dominant term, and
death had been comprehended by life. Following Hiroshima —
that awesome, tragic, and paradoxically catalytic event — a
reversal occurred within the fundamental relationship: death
became the commanding term, and life was conceived in terms
of death, first for those directly affected by the war, but
gradually for an increasingly larger number of people.

With this came changes in the ways human beings understood both themselves and the world in which they live.

Humans came to conceive of life differently, and the ramifications were felt in various aspects of their common life. People related to people, and nations to nations, in a different way. Changes came in attitudes toward government, leadership, the role of the military, and all forms and reservoirs of power, even authority itself. From this point forward, all instruments of power, in degrees never before possible, were approached with suspicion. Power by definition carried the threat of destruction, and destruction had the capacity for extinction.

Lifton used this interpretation to describe how patterns of personality formation changed from a fixed to a fluid, protean style. Sensitivities nurtured by such awareness called for an urgent and thorough reexamination of everything upon which sustained human life depends. We reassessed the function of our dominant political, social, and cultural institutions, giving serious attention to the dynamics of world order, particularly as these had been changed by the cataclysmic event of Hiroshima. The function and value of education had to be, and were, reassessed. Value issues, many of which were assumed to have been settled long ago, were opened to fresh examination. There was deep recognition that the survival of the species required deliberate attention.

Further, given the radical and primary character of the change that had occurred, there was no assurance that new strategies would prove successful. Indeed, strategy itself became a subject of critical attention. It was as if the forces that had been unleashed were too powerful to be tamed and were threatening to run their own courses, challenged only, as Thomas Merton said, by "an alternative way of being." Along the way an accumulation of wondrous scientific advances would make the prospect of all-out destruction more immediate and imminent.

And it was not simply Hiroshima; it was also the Holocaust that brought about these changes. The two events became fused in Western consciousness. Ron Rosenbaum described this coupling as follows:

When early strategists began to talk about the
totality of nuclear war, they used phrases like "the
death of consciousness" on the planet. Kissinger used
the only slightly more modest phrase "an end to
history." Without consciousness, not only is there no
history, there is no sorrow, no pain, no remorse. No
one is missing or missed. There is nothing to feel bad
about because nothing exists to feel. A death so total
becomes almost communal. The Holocaust of the European Jews left behind millions to feel horror,
bitterness, and loss. When people began applying the
world "holocaust" to nuclear war they meant a holocaust with no survivors, or one in which, to use the
well-known phrase, "the survivors would envy the
dead." Even now when a much-disputed scientific
report argues the probability for long-term post-
holocaust survival, at least in the southern hemi-
sphere, one does not, if one is an American, think of
surviving a total nuclear war. One thinks of dying in a
flash before there's time to feel the pain. Could that be
the attraction, if that word may be used, of nuclear
war? Is there some Keatsian element "half in love with
easeful death" in our fantasies of the end?[2]

In many respects Hiroshima created Vietnam. The revised
understanding of the implications of warfare affected the way
the Vietnam War was perceived, interpreted, portrayed, and
fought. Because the stakes were conceived differently, the war
was regulated by a new agenda. Winning and losing could not
mean what they meant before; neither could be determined on
the basis of the acquisition of territory, the winning of battles,
the killing of enemy soldiers, the bombing of enemy establishments, the plundering of enemy strongholds. The battles were
motivated by other kinds of interests and were assessed by new
criteria; the battlefield was the arena wherein other sorts of
conflict were finding dramatic expression. The issue was not
simply physical combat, nor could differences of opinion be
restricted to matters of military strategy.

Vietnam became both the scene and the testing ground for
a comprehensive adjustment of human priorities. Some of the

sensitivities nurtured in response to Hiroshima and the Jewish Holocaust could not find simultaneous enunciation and challenge until Vietnam. By the time of the Vietnam War, Hiroshima's realignments had become self-conscious and had come to influence strategy. This made it impossible to judge the outcome of the war in traditional terms. The threat of destruction of infinite proportions was the regulative term by which all finite events were given a corresponding place.

Signs of this large transposition appear in American religious attitudes. It is no longer necessary to demonstrate that the years since the early 1960s have seen a phenomenal growth of interest in spiritual religion in the West. Yoga, transcendental meditation, transpersonal psychology, psychic awareness, mind-expanding experiences, and the attraction of Eastern gurus are examples. No less significant is the development of a simpler, less conflicted attitude or response to life—an orientation that is being nurtured in the West in part through the influence of Asian religious currents. These are facts of modern religious, social, cultural, and psychological experience.

However, the link between this religious transformation and the Vietnam War has not been thoroughly appreciated. Vietnam eased the way toward recognition of the power of Asian religious sensibility, a set of self-consistent religious and attitudinal possibilities to which the West had been made susceptible by the gnawing experience of Hiroshima.

This proposal does not depend upon any simple-minded influence theory. It does not mean that those westerners who went to Vietnam were exposed to Asia simply by being there, then returned, bringing the treasures back with them. Some of this happened, of course. But the linkage is more specific. Vietnam was fought in the Occident as well as in the Orient, and the terms were as much mental, psychological, and spiritual as geographical and military. Vietnam stimulated Asian religious sensitivities in the West because it could not be adequately or satisfactorily comprehended in the most prominent and/or standard Western ideational terms.

Dietrich Bonhoeffer, the German Protestant theologian who met his death on the gallows in a Nazi prison in 1945, would have understood the connections. In words not wholly legible from his *Letters and Papers from Prison*, he suggests that the occurrence of two full-scale world wars in Europe in less than half a century was a judgment of the severest kind against the Christian religion. Bonhoeffer perceived that there is something intrinsic to the spirit of Western religion which allows and perhaps encourages such conflict. He was pointing to a dispositional factor, which is not to overlook the prominent injunctions to love one's enemies and to turn the other cheek, refusing to respond in kind when one is despised, harmed, or wrongfully used. Nor is it to minimize Christianity's emphasis upon love, peace, brotherhood, harmony, and gentleness — qualities that are vividly exemplified in the lives of St. Francis of Assisi, Mother Teresa of Calcutta, and many other well- and lesser-known people.

Bonhoeffer's point does recognize, however, that the religions entrenched in Western culture are primarily father religions, and father religions characteristically are (to use David Bakan's words) religions of agency. They encourage one to set things in motion, to be an effective doer, to work for a particular cause or objective. Only with great reluctance will they accept things as they are. Indeed, they work to make things better. They are instrumental. They channel and regulate power. They seek goals not yet achieved.

This kind of aggressive, antipassive mood or disposition in religions of agency finds it fitting that there is an ultimate victory. It encourages the promotion of strategies through which good will redress, eliminate, or conquer evil. It believes it proper that right should vanquish wrong and that justice should be effected, even though it provides considerable latitude regarding the means by which this shall occur. All this belongs to a conviction that life does indeed exhibit a basic propriety, a fundamental harmony, a sense of balance and rightness that wishes to be exercised, must be enunciated, and eventually must become visible. Even the great song of the social revolution of the 1960s, "We Shall Overcome," can be understood in these terms.

Vietnam was a severe challenge to these fundamental convictions, because it provided no clear way in which victory could be conceived or its terms enacted. Right and wrong could not be clearly distinguished; the components of justice could not be easily identified. In religious terms, the event did not seem to exhibit a theophanous character, as Paul Tillich would have put it; it was difficult to construe the day-by-day occurrences as visible signs of the working of an invisible divine will.

Hiroshima was a precursor, for it created the compulsion thoroughly to revise the implications of warfare. But Hiroshima was more than this; it also brought, with remarkable force, an awareness of the imminence of the end to consciousness. The response has been apocalyptic. Two of the potential outcomes are Armageddon and Eden.

Morris Dickstein places the chain of developments in a sequential pattern in his analysis of contemporary American culture, *Gates of Eden: American Culture in the Sixties*:

> The fifties were a great period for home and family, for getting and spending, for cultivating one's garden. All that is reflected in its writing. But its spokesmen also called it an Age of Anxiety; behind its material growth hovers a quiet despair, whose symbols are the Bomb and the still-vivid death camps, and a fear of Armageddon . . . But this anxiety is metaphysical and hermetic, closed in upon itself . . .
>
> The spirit of the sixties witnessed the transformation of utopian religion into the terms of secular humanism . . . So the sixties translated the Edenic impulse once again into political terms . . . starting with the civil-rights movement, which was propelled by the millennial spirit of Southern black religion . . .
>
> The culture of the fifties was European in its irony and sophistication. It put its faith in what is called "the tragic sense of life," a fateful determinism that affirmed the obduracy of man's nature and his surroundings. But for the culture of the sixties the watchword was *liberation*: the shackles of tradition and

circumstance were to be thrown off, society was to be molded to the shape of human possibility.

By the early seventies . . . time had once again revealed to us the illusion and even dangers of "paradise now," and had disclosed virtues we had slighted . . .

Then, with particular reference to Vietnam, Dickstein continues:

I needn't apply such subtle reasoning to the collapse of our client state in Vietnam to show that it too belonged among the unfinished business of the sixties. In Vietnam we lost not only a war and a subcontinent; we also lost our pervasive confidence that American arms and American aims were linked somehow to justice and morality, not merely to the quest for power. America was defeated militarily, but the "idea" of America, the cherished myth of America, received an even more shattering blow.[3]

The chronicle Dickstein weaves carries compelling interpretive force. The awareness of the imminence of the end time explicit in the Hiroshima aftermath translated simultaneously into both threat and opportunity. The event transposes heaven and hell, as Ernst Bloch said, into real possibilities. From the one side, there is a well-founded fear of cataclysmic annihilation of the human race. But the same conditions, from the same analysis, can also stimulate a "paradise now" campaign. Both readings – indeed, the composite reading – are in keeping with a Christian interpretation of the meaning of history. The entire chronicle can be incorporated within the dominant American religious framework. For all of it there are precedents and analogues. It is Armageddon or it is Eden. All of it makes sense in these terms – all of it, that is, until Vietnam. The experience of Vietnam breaks the interpretive framework; it is a profound "category error," a severe challenge to the mythological sequence.

The Vietnam War fostered many of the same insights that are taught in Asian religious traditions, particularly in Buddhism. In suggesting this, we are drawing upon the consensus of scholars from Max Weber on that religious traditions can be distinguished on the basis of their characteristic uses, expres-

sions, and legitimization of power. They will dispose themselves differently on such topics as the meaning of success and
failure; they will evaluate and define winning and losing differently. All religions will devote fundamental attention to questions about the appropriate ranges of human agency, the nature
of true humility, differences between activity and passivity,
and how each of these should be valued. All will provide counsel as to how to live with the experience of loss. How the traditions treat these and related topics provides a clear indication of
how they mark the relationship between sacred and profane.

In a provocative book, *The Nobility of Failure*, Ivan Morris
approaches the concept of heroism against this background.
Though his distinctions are overdrawn, his portrayal is instructive. He writes:

> The Judeo-Christian approach is based on the
> comforting idea that, so long as a man keeps faith,
> God will be on his side and he, or at least his cause,
> will eventually triumph. Thus, a hero like Roland,
> though defeated in battle, is never abandoned by God
> and succeeds in contributing to the Christian victory
> over the Saracens.
> This basically optimistic outlook has been
> especially conspicuous in the most Western of all
> major Western countries, the United States of Amer-
> ica, whose tradition has always tended to extrude any
> tragic sense of life and, often against cogent evidence
> to the contrary, to put its trust in the essential good-
> ness of mankind, or at least that part of mankind
> which is fortunate enough to reside within its bounda-
> ries. "I know America," a recent President was fond of
> saying, "and the heart of America is good." The state-
> ment is not without a certain irony when one recalls
> the identity of its author; yet the sentiment reflects an
> underlying assumption that has been widely and con-
> fidently accepted. Americans, of course, are no
> strangers to despair; yet it comes not from any philo-
> sophical awareness of man's existential limitations but
> from disappointment that follows excessive hope in
> the possibility of compassing worldly happiness.

By contrast, Morris describes an attitude toward life that has been expressed in Japanese culture and is typical of the Buddhist orientation.

> At the opposite end of the spectrum are the Japanese, who since ancient times have tended to resign themselves to the idea that the world and the human condition are *not* essentially benign. For all the country's vigor and ebullience, there is a deep strain of natural pessimism, a sense that ultimately things are against us and that, however hard we may strive, we are involved in a losing game. Sooner or later each individual is doomed to fail; for, even if he may over-come the multifarious hurdles set by a harsh society, he will finally be defeated by the natural powers of age, illness, and death. Human life . . . is full of sad vicissitudes, fleeting, impermanent like the seasons. Helplessness and failure are built into human enterprises.[4]

Morris says that this underlying pessimism, which also recognizes a wonderful beauty and poignancy in "the pathos of things," is supported by Mahayana Buddhist religion.

The linkages between this orientation and the lessons of Vietnam are subtle and indirect. Through the frustrations of the Vietnam experience came a strong need for Americans to make sense of things without recourse to the fundamentally opti-mistic, happiness- and success-dominated outlook of the West. James Dittes, a Yale University psychologist, refers to this as the search for the grammar of "positive disengagement." This need in turn directed attention to sources of individual and corporate authority that counseled repression and extinction rather than cultivation of the acquisitive, regressive, agential posture. One of the lessons of the Vietnam experience was that conflict derives from acquisitive impulses and can never be resolved by the satisfaction of desire, because satisfactions simply stimulate additional desires. What is required instead is abolition, negation, repression, a quenching of appetite, and a deepened empathy with what Morris calls "the pathos of worldly misfortune."

The basis of this recognition is to be found virtually wherever one looks within Buddhist literature. The Dharma-sangiti Sutra, for example, expresses it this way:

> He who maintains the doctrine of Emptiness is not allured by the things of the world, because they have no basis. He is not excited by gain or dejected by loss. Fame does not dazzle him and infamy does not shame him. Scorn does not repel him, praise does not attract him. Pleasure does not please him, pain does not trouble him. He who is not allured by the things of the world knows Emptiness, and one who maintains the doctrine of Emptiness has neither likes nor dislikes. What he likes he knows to be only Emptiness and sees it as such.[5]

Alan Watts, who has had much to do with introducing westerners to Buddhist thought and sensitivity, offers this explanation:

> Perhaps I can express this Buddhist fascination for the mystery of nothingness in another way. If we get rid of all wishful thinking and dubious metaphysical speculations, we can hardly doubt that–at a time not too distant–each one of us will simply cease to be. It won't be like going into darkness forever, for there will be neither darkness, nor time, nor sense of futility, nor anyone to feel anything about it . . . The universe will, supposedly, be going on as usual, but for each individual it will be as if it had never happened at all; and even that is saying too much, because there won't be anyone for whom it never happened.
> Make this prospect as real as possible: the one total certainty. You will be as if you had never existed, which was, however, the way you were before you did exist–and not only you but everything else. Nevertheless, with such an improbable past, here we are. We begin from nothing and end in nothing . . . Think it over and over, trying to conceive the fact of coming to never having existed . . .
> All of a sudden it will strike you that this nothing-ness is the most potent, magical, basic, and reliable thing you ever thought of, and that the reason you can't form the slightest idea of it is that it's yourself. But not the self you thought you were.[6]

Allen Ginsberg recalls his religious conversion, while riding on the train en route to Tokyo from Kyoto in 1963, in a poem called "Change":

> In the midst of the broken consciousness of mid twentieth century anguish of separation from my own body and its natural infirmity of feeling its own self one with all self, I instinctively seeking to reconstitute that blissful union which I experienced so rarely that I took it to be supernatural and gave it holy Name thus made hymn lament of longing and litanies of trium-phancy of Self over the mind-illusion mechano-universe of un-feeling Time in which I saw my self my own mother and my very nature trapped.[7]

It was out of this temper of experience that people sought a basis for ending the war in Vietnam. This required the discovery of an alternative strategy by which the dominant expectation would be held up to scrutiny and the natural pro-pensity for winning, for victory, would be dissolved or redirected. Gradually, but in a visibly stumbling manner, the nation's leaders came to see this, but they could not find the language or the appropriate sanctions. Occasionally they came close, only to fall back into grand hyperbole about the demonic character of the enemy, but to no avail. They wound down the war effort, only to pump it up to full force again. In the end, however, it was disengagement they wanted to effect, and they found access through a lexicon developed within Asian reli-gious settings.

Significantly, growing nuclear sensitivity, war pathos, the birth of the counterculture, and a Western awakening to the power of Asian religious sensitivity happened together and at once. The pathway toward Eastern religions had been prepared by the writings of Ginsberg, Watts, D. T. Suzuki, Thomas Merton, the San Francisco poets, several historians and philos-ophers of religion, and, of course, by an increasing number of opportunities for cultural contact and exchange. Given the strong currents already under way, the Vietnam War played only a catalytic role.

Colin Wilson defines an *outsider* as one who has broken the circuit of the prevailing way of life and now stands apart, pushed there by the utter strangeness of the folkways of the dominant society. In other words, the outsider is a person who feels he can no longer live in the comfortable, insulated world, merely accepting what he sees and touches as substantial and dependable. He has come to see the illusions too clearly and to feel the pathos too keenly, and thus comes under an obligation to go away to some abode beyond unreality's control and jurisdiction.[8]

The Vietnam experience encouraged large numbers of individuals to become "outsiders," and eventually contemplatives. The stories such people tell about themselves and the attitudes they have adopted indicate that they no longer feel at one with the environment in which they were nurtured. They have learned through experience, and indeed to their sadness, that the America that once was – if it ever was – is no longer. They have found that the transmitted creeds are too simplistic to enable them to come effectively to terms with the world's disorder and pervasive disharmony. The "outsiders" know that virtue hardly ever falls out along "good guy versus bad guy" lines, that the issues over which wars are fought can be defended from either side, depending on where one stands, and that truth and error are rarely discernible within adversarial frameworks. As a consequence, they have begun worrying less about dogma and religious institutions and more about self-knowledge and disciplined self-consciousness.

It is understandable that westerners would try to flee beyond now proven illusions toward a more substantial reality that might be found within the individual, and predictable that they would come to regard inner or spiritual reality as solely dependable. For a host of good reasons, they found the Asian religious traditions supportive of their quest.

Certainly the West was not without contemplative resources of its own, but through the years, for the most part, this dimension of religion had not been stressed. When the shared enlightenment occurred, westerners began probing the literature and devotional manuals of the Judeo-Christian tradition for analogues and parallels to what they had found in the East, rediscovering the mystical writings of Meister Eckhart, Jan van Ruysbroeck, and Richard Rolle, and especially *The Cloud of Unknowing*. They made new acquaintance with Western monastic life, particularly those forms touched by the influence of Thomas Merton, a Trappist monk who explored the writings of Zen Buddhism and died on a pilgrimage to Asia. It was appropriate that many of the "outsiders" found themselves on the monastic trail, for monks have been the perennial advocates of counterculture in the West.

Still, such interests do not imply that those so inclined used such newly found sanctions to exit completely from social and political responsibility. On the contrary, many of them moved beyond partisan and sectarian allegiances toward envisioning the plight of the world as a whole. A strong interest in exercising global responsibility surfaced, and it was out of the same network of recognitions, in the years immediately following the cessation of military hostilities in Vietnam, that a new peace movement developed on an international scale. As could have been expected, the movement advocated global harmony, making contemplative aspirations fundamental to its incentives.

Predictably, too, there was reaction from those who also experienced the disillusion but responded differently to it. Many within Western society recommended a return to a resolute mutual support of traditional religious and patriotic allegiances.

7. Right to Armageddon

"We believe that America, the last stronghold of faith on this planet, has come under increasing attack from Satan's forces in recent years."

— FROM "STATEMENT OF PURPOSE,"
The Christian Voice

WHEN MORRIS DICKSTEIN writes about the principal social and cultural characteristics of American life in the 1960s, he has ample basis upon which to contrast the symbolism of Eden and Armageddon. Following the birth of the thermonuclear age, the collective fears and anxieties of the fifties can be typified in Armageddon imagery, which speaks of the expectation of the cataclysmic end of human history. Dickstein notes that the sixties turned attention to the other side, the possibilities implicit in the recovery of a lost Eden. Instead of viewing the future as an occasion of foreboding, the Edenic impulse revived hopes and dreams of an ideal age. Illustration of this reversal is found in the heralding of the Great Society, the birth of the "flower children," efforts toward emancipation from oppression, and the basic confidence that the challenges facing the American people (poverty, hunger, economic stability, equality of opportunity) could be successfully met.[1]

It is instructive to consider that many important developments in American life in the 1970s, particularly in the post-Vietnam years, involved another reversal—that is, a return from Edenic aspirations to the mind-set of Armageddon. The strong reemergence of conservative religion, with its determined enunciation of fundamentalist themes, is evidence of this, as is the more widespread expectation among Americans that the nation is headed for decisive military engagement which, in the thermonuclear age, may have all of the cataclysmic and catastrophic elements of Armageddon. Americans understand that a "war to end all wars" has not yet occurred but may be imminent.

The means of access to this mental attitude lies within the apocalyptic mode, which, as we have suggested, is encouraged by the inversion of expectations that occurs when interpretive frameworks are broken and self-consistent, overarching meaning becomes inaccessible. Such challenges to rightful expectation were fundamental to American collective experience in Vietnam, and hence the resulting intrinsically apocalyptic dependence upon the products of the imagination, fantasies and dreams has led to Armageddon in the post-Vietnam era. The rebirth of the mood carries resonance, particularly when we place it within the context of the collective disappointment over the outcome of the war that has surfaced in the postwar years.

The American situation was ripe, it seems, for the creation of movements such as the Moral Majority and the host of political interest groups that share its purposes. Without question, this religious and political development bears clear and direct linkages with the Vietnam War. Indeed, the revival of militaristic talk, the expectation of an impending battle, the interdependent commitments to strong conservative religion and to a strong national defense, and the fusion of patriotic zeal with religious fervor – so inseparably that each virtually stands for the other – constitute unambiguous testimony that the Vietnam War is unfinished and that many (the silent majority, perhaps?) find it impossible to live with its ambivalent preliminary outcome.

This significant national development has come to be symbolized by the work of Dr. Jerry Falwell, principal pastor of Thomas Road Baptist Church in Lynchburg, Virginia, and titular head of the Moral Majority. Falwell's sermons on the "Old Time Gospel Hour" on television commend "Jesus First" as well as a return to the convictions of the nation's founding fathers. Through them all flows the evangelistic preacher's resentment over the weakened position to which the United States has fallen, evident in the sorry plight of Americans in their indecisive confrontation with communism in Vietnam.

While delineating his agenda for the eighties, Jerry Falwell offers several observations on America's experience in the Vietnam War, not simply to analyze the war's effects but to provide a prescription for the ills he perceives to be most crucial at this point in American history. Predictably, he mentions the network of "family issues" first, decrying the increased divorce rate and the breakdown of the American family as a reliable institution. He reiterates his "pro-life" and "pro-traditional family" convictions, his opposition to abortion, pornography, illegal drug traffic, sex education in the public schools, and homosexuality, and his repulsion for the influences of humanistic philosophy (frequently called secular humanism) upon churches, schools, and society at large. Within the same list of negatives he declares his unqualified support of a strong defense. "A strong national defense is the best deterrent to war, " he states. "The only way America can remain free is to remain strong."[2]

Falwell's prescriptions follow his personal conviction about the status and stature of America as a nation founded "under God." He concedes that the United States is not perfect; he cautions that it would be a great mistake to equate America with the kingdom of God. Repeatedly stating that he is absolutely opposed to the establishment of a Christian theocracy in America, he yet wishes to affirm that America is "without question the greatest nation on the face of God's earth," a nation conceived according to principles that insure God's blessing.[3] Falwell recognizes, of course, that not all the founding fathers were Christians as he would prefer to use that identification, yet even those who were not – even the deists – were following convictions compatible with Falwell's conservative Christianity. The nation was established as a grand experiment in democratic participatory government in which the law (instead of the state or the monarch) held supremacy. Those "certain inalienable rights" that the founding fathers enunciated were not granted by the state, but belonged to the authority understood to come from God.

The current threat to this sense of things, in Falwell's eyes, comes from an evil force that manifests itself in a variety of forms, all of which carry the same debilitating power. First of all, Falwell is concerned about the deterioration of America's moral fiber. The primary institution of the society, the family, is severely threatened. Forty percent of all U.S. marriages end in divorce; children, following the eviscerating influences of television—which invites "porno-poisoners" to do their work—are victimized by purveyors of the alien sense of life and thus become easy prey for those who make profit in drug traffic.

Furthermore, according to Falwell, the sense of patriotism is for the most part absent from American collective sensibilities, largely because of the work of government. Government-supported sex education in the schools usurps the rights of parents to tell their children about the sanctity of sexuality; the Supreme Court decision to legalize abortions opened the floodgates to promiscuity, which in turn militates against the stability of the family. The feminist movement, in Falwell's view, is also working to increase the deterioration of the family and the home, and the growing acceptance of homosexuality is a dramatic concomitant of the same debilitating and disorienting tendencies. America as a nation is in danger of losing its moral character. It is sliding down the slippery road toward collective decay and disintegration from within.

Falwell talks about these developments while renouncing the evils of secular humanism, the godless philosophy being taught and promoted in the public schools. It is a philosophy that preaches evolutionism as the scientific explanation of how the world came to be; it gives no place to the viewpoint that the Christian God is the creator of the universe and has a specific plan for the life of each of his creatures. Secular humanism enthrones man, placing him at the center of existence. Falwell believes that it has become the dominant and sole philosophy through which the public schools inform the thinking and shape the lives of their students. Each time it is successful, it fashions a human being who stands in opposition to, or at least in tension with, the Christian religious perspective. Through its influence homes are broken, families are brought to ruin, and individuals come to look to the state, to government, to provide their needs.

These developments, Falwell believes, are responsible for encouraging the largest and most formidable direct threat to American vitality—the possibility that our established and cherished way of life will be supplanted by an alternative form of government which will accord the opposing sense of life supremacy. Falwell understands the deterioration of the collective reality to be occurring in successive stages: first, moral decay from within; next, invasion by socialist forces, from both within and without; finally, if the socialist tendency is not thwarted, collective reality organized according to the incentives of the Communist state. In this last stage, the opposing force by which the society is most severely threatened becomes the motivating force by which the society is governed. Falwell's implication is that those who wish to preserve or restore the American way of life must watch for both internal and external threats; the latter in particular require the maintenance of a robust military posture.

Wishing to influence the nation's actions during the 1980s, Falwell warns that the military might of the United States has been decreasing in comparison with that of the Soviet Union. If this tendency is allowed to continue unchecked, there is a very real possibility that America will be forced to surrender its vital freedoms. As he puts it:

> America is in serious trouble today. It has lost its economic and military prominence among the nations of the world. Exercising influence and leadership from this weakened position is an exercise in futility. Our leaders are finally realizing what many have tried to state for years: that the Soviets are liars and cheaters, and that they are determined to conquer our free country and to infiltrate the American people.[4]

Falwell takes some comfort from the fact that the leadership of the country is becoming more aware of this awful situation and has initiated steps to reverse the trend. On more than one occasion he has said privately that Ronald Reagan is "the best thing to happen to this country in twenty years."

When Falwell reaches out to military authority for support of his analyses, he characteristically turns to the essays of General Lewis Walt, particularly to *The Eleventh Hour*, in which Walt contends that the United States could easily fall to the power of the Soviet Union. If the Soviet Union chose to place the American people under "an oligarchy of tyrants whose viciousness and brutality have no match in that long, bloody history of man's cruelty," it could do so; in General Walt's view, the United States simply has no way of preventing such an occurrence. "Today the U.S. has no civil-defense program, no antiballistic missiles, and no appreciable defense against even a bomber attack. This stripping of our defense forces has been a deliberate policy move of our civilian defense officials."[5]

When one of the two nations is weak or benign and the other is bent on world conquest, the weak one has no chance. Falwell is certain that communism is committed to taking over the world, pursuing this ambition by encouraging the forces that transform a capitalist into a socialist society. Communism needs socialism to provide social adhesion. Falwell knows when it happens; indeed, the developments are clear to anyone willing to observe. "Churches are shut down, preachers are killed and imprisoned, and Bibles are taken away from the people," he explained in a sermon. When this happens, the possibility that the world might be evangelized – which Falwell finds both his own and the church's purpose – becomes severely diminished.

Falwell has provided an expanded published statement on these subjects in his book *Listen America!*, published in 1980. Here he expresses the same fears about pornography, homosexuality, sexual immorality on network television, the breakdown of family relationships, rock music, drugs, alcohol, Affirmative Action legislation, the feminist revolution, the Equal Rights Amendment, and the rising but adverse power of secular humanism, surveying each of these topics in a comprehensive diagnosis of America's prevailing illness. But the major problem is that the nation has departed from its original understanding of the fundamental relationship it enjoys with God. It no longer consciously or deliberately perceives itself as a nation "under God."

"God promoted America to a greatness no other nation has ever enjoyed because her heritage is one of a republic governed by laws predicated on the Bible," Falwell declares.[6] But this originating vision is no longer the prevailing attitude. Consequently, there are dark clouds on America's horizon, and time is running out. Soon there may be no opportunity to return to the principles implicit in the "basics" upon which America was founded. Yet "if Americans will face the truth, our nation can be turned around and saved from the evils and destruction that have fallen upon every other nation that has turned its back on God."[7]

When he launches into this portion of his prophetic message, Falwell likes to compare the perils of the present time with the situation he knew as a boy in Campbell County, Virginia. He remembers hikes in the woods, schoolboy athletics, and the fun-loving pranks he and his classmates played upon their teachers. He recalls what it was like to be interested in girls and remembers with appreciation the counsel given him by older members of the community. He even looks back with considerable thankfulness to listening to his radio in his bedroom. While recounting this list of memories, he easily adds:

> I remember the time when it was positive to be patriotic, and as far as I am concerned, it still is. I remember as a boy, when the flag was raised, everyone stood proudly and put his hand upon his heart and pledged allegiance with gratitude. I remember when the band struck up "The Stars and Stripes Forever," we stood and goose pimples would run all over me. I remember when I was in elementary school during World War II, when every report from the other shores meant something to us. We were not out there demonstrating against our guys who were dying

in Europe and Asia. We were praying for them and thanking God for them and buying war bonds to help pay for the materials and artillery they needed to fight and win and come back.[8]

Falwell yearns for a return to the same feeling, to the same sense of life and the same priorities, and he recognizes that he is not alone in this. Indeed, he senses that he has the sentiment of the majority of Americans, in spite of the fact that not all of them are professed Christians, on his side. Thus he can state baldly: "I believe that Americans want to see this country come back to basics, back to values, back to Biblical morality, back to sensibility, and back to patriotism."[9]

In sum, his message is that the situation is serious and time is passing, but the opportunity to rectify it has not passed away, and Americans do not have to allow it to slip from firm grasp. "Today, more than at any time in history, America needs men and women of God who have an understanding of the times and are not afraid to stand up for what is right. We are not a perfect nation, but we are still a free nation because we have the blessing of God upon us. We must continue to follow in a path that will ensure that blessing. We must not forget that it is God Almighty who has made and preserved us as a nation."[10]

He puts the same in slightly different words:

Americans must no longer linger in ignorance and apathy. We cannot be silent about the sins that are destroying this nation. The choice is ours. We must turn America around or prepare for inevitable destruction. I am listening to the sounds that threaten to take away our liberties in America. And I have listened to God's admonitions and his direction—the only hopes of saving America.[11]

Through his enunciation, Falwell is tough on communism and even more pointed in his opposition to the Soviet Union. Communism is godless and materialistic. It transposes allegiances from God to the state. It works to obliterate spirituality, tending instead to emphasize a quantitative appraisal of human life. What bothers Falwell even more is that the Communist system of government, based upon the convictions of atheistic materialism and devoid of belief in the afterlife, has been determined from the time of Lenin on to dominate the world. Its tactic, to insert socialism in places where capitalism previously ruled, occurs when a country's military strength is weakened and its morals corrupted "so that its people have no will to resist wrong."[12]

Falwell believes that his hatred of communism can be justified both religiously and politically. He sees Communists as "bloodthirsty marauding rapists, looters, killers, who mercilessly chop off people's heads, and have murdered one hundred forty-seven million people, at last count, since the Bolshevik Revolution in 1917."[13] Americans are not sufficiently alert any longer to the menace, and too many of those who have attempted to point out the seriousness of the situation have been branded as alarmists. Falwell comments: "Americans have been silent much too long. We have stood by and watched as American power and influence have been systematically weakened in every sphere of the world."[14]

The Vietnam War is an important contributing factor to this attitude. In Falwell's view, the problem in Vietnam was that the United States tried to conduct a "no-win war." He supports the statement made by J. Edgar Hoover, late director of the FBI, who warned: "We are at war with communism and the sooner every red-blooded American can realize this, the safer we will be." Falwell adds: "But it appears that America's policy toward communism is one of containment, rather than victory."[15]

Referring to a father who complained to the U.S. Defense Department that his son was out in Vietnam "fighting a no-win war with limited political objectives," Falwell asserts that the boy was "fighting a war with one hand tied behind his back." He agrees with the father's assessment that this is "a miserable way to fight a war."[16] He agrees too with a statement by James R. Schlesinger, then U.S. secretary of defense, to the effect that the United States lost in Vietnam because it did not use its military power.

People close to Jerry Falwell have said that on occasion he has expressed doubts about whether the United States should ever have become involved in Vietnam in the first place, but notwithstanding these doubts, his dominant attitude is that once it was involved, the nation was under an obligation to win.

The war in Vietnam, then, serves as symbol of America's ineffectiveness and the progressively weakening character of its moral resolve. Indeed, America's experience in Vietnam belongs in a series with the decay of family life, the disintegration of shared values and aspirations, and an inability effectively to counter the relentless onrush of those forces that threaten to undo it.

At about this point in his litany of failures, Falwell again offers gratitude to God that time hasn't run out completely and there is still an opportunity to reverse these debilitating trends. He can say it this way:

> It is God Almighty who has made and preserved us as a nation, and the day we forget that is the day the United States will become a byword among the nations of the world. We will become nothing more than a memory in a history book, like the many great civilizations that have preceded us.

Or he can say it this way:

> America's only hope for survival is a spiritual awakening that begins in the lives of her individual citizens. It is only in the spiritual rebirth of our nation's citizens that we can have a positive hope in the future.[17]

Or in such phrases as this:

> I do not believe that God is finished with America yet. America has more God-fearing citizens per capita than any other nation on earth.

Or with this plea for a new commitment:

> Against the growing tide of permissiveness and moral decay that is crushing our society, we must make a sacred commitment to God Almighty to turn this nation around immediately.[18]

These themes are present in almost everything Jerry Falwell says and writes. Providing a defense of his views for *Newsweek* on September 21, 1981, he stated that he represents people who are pro-American, adding that this "means that we stand for a strong national defense, believing that freedom is the ultimate issue." When he listed the seven basic principles of Judeo-Christian society—the seven basic principles that made America great—he pointed out that ours is a nation under God which in recent years has violated "the principle of divine establishments." When he organized the first "I Love America" rally on the steps of the United States Capitol, with congressional delegates participating, he intended to return the country to "moral sanity" by reversing the social, political, and spiritual trends that had gained force during the Vietnam era.

Falwell also defends his affiliation with the Moral Majority (a group he helped found, and which he insists is a political, not a religious, organization) by talking about his responsibilities as a minister of the Gospel, compelled to speak in a prophetic voice. When he explains how Thomas Road Baptist Church became the sponsor of the national "I Love America" rallies, he speaks of his sense that the world is living in the final generation before the return of the Messiah. And when one of his close associates was asked if Dr. Falwell truly wishes the whole world to become Christian, thus obliterating Hindus, Buddhists, Jews, Muslims, Sikhs, and others, the response was, "Yes, but he's realistic. He knows that this will not happen until the Messiah returns."

The temper of Falwell's message is apocalyptic and intense. Not only does he describe the forces in the world in black-and-white, absolute terms, as though they were in a fight to the finish, but he declares that the contest in which they are engaged is in its final stages and will be resolved within a very short while. More significantly, everything in the world has meaning only to the extent that it can be fitted into this full-scale conflict between absolute forces. There can be no real recourse to pastoral tranquillity, not even the kind which rural Campbell County, Virginia, boasts, because the aggressor has initiated his moves and his intentions are relentless. We are involved in a fight to the finish. Christians must fit themselves for battle, for the conflict is already under way all around them.

Within this context, it becomes appropriate for Falwell to describe the work of the church in military terms: "The local church is an organized army equipped for battle, ready to charge the enemy. The Sunday School is the attacking squad. The church should be a disciplined, charging army. Christians, like slaves and soldiers, ask no questions."[19] Then, describing the work that Christians are to perform in evangelizing the world, Falwell makes the military analogy even more explicit:

> It is important to bombard the territory, to move out near the coast and shell the enemy. It is important to send in the literature. It is important to send that radio broadcast and to use that dial-a-prayer telephone. It is important to have all those external forces being set loose on the enemy's stronghold.
>
> But ultimately some Marines have to march in, encounter the enemy face to face, and put the flag up, that is, build the local church.
>
> I'm speaking of Marines who have been called of God to move in past the shelling, the bombing and the foxholes and, with bayonet in hand, encounter the enemy face to face and one-on-one bring them under submission to the Gospel of Christ, move them into the household of God, put up the flag and call it secured.[20]

The final line is one Jerry Falwell employs frequently in finishing a sermon or bringing an injunction to resolution: "You and I are called to occupy until He comes." (James Watt, secretary of the interior under President Reagan, has quoted this phrase too when defending his attitude toward the use of land and natural resources.)

Falwell's attitudes are significant not simply because he is pastor of a church with a membership of twenty thousand, a television evangelist for a program with the busiest WATS line in the United States, and the head of the Moral Majority. They are significant because they represent the general feeling of a

host of groups – Christian Voice, Christian Legal Assistance
Society, National Christian Action Coalition, Religious Roundtable, and others – with strong and sometimes effective political
arms. The national elections of November 1980 witnessed the
ability of "the Falwell phenomenon" to defeat liberal U.S. Senators George McGovern in South Dakota, John Culver in Iowa,
Birch Bayh in Indiana, and Frank Church in Idaho – among the
congressmen who were most effective in ending America's
involvement in the Vietnam War.

Some of Falwell's fellows espouse a more open and resolute militancy; for instance, Falwell's associate Tim LaHaye,
founder of the San Diego Christian Unified School System and
Christian Heritage College, takes up the cause in his book,
appropriately titled *The Battle for the Mind*. In LaHaye's view,
Americans, particularly those of a fundamentalist Christian
persuasion, are locked in battle against a relentless foe. It isn't
simply communism this time, although communism is always
involved; it is secular humanism, the growing tendency within
society to try to solve human problems without drawing upon
divine resources.

LaHaye believes that moral conditions within the country
have worsened in direct proportion to humanism's influence.
U.S. society is no longer based upon Biblical principles, but has
become amoral, with little or no recollection that it was established under a covenant. In LaHaye's view, the only force
capable of halting humanism in its tracks is the church of Jesus
Christ. The opposing force is the socialist conspiracy, which
utilizes the mechanisms of the United Nations, the World
Health Organization, and other agencies sponsored by "one-
worlders" to effect a socialist revolution by the year 2000.
Socialism is also responsible for transforming "the most powerful country in the world after World War II into a neutralized
state," permitting the Soviet Union to make socialist prisons out
of its satellite countries in Eastern Europe, turning Cuba into a
Russian armed camp, and preventing the United States from

winning in Korea and in Vietnam and from retaining the Panama Canal.

The church must rise up to challenge the enemy: "It is time that the 110,000 faithful ministers from every Bible-believing denomination in our country lead the 60 million Christians to vote out of office every devotee of humanism and every politician naive enough to vote for humanist programs." In different words: "It has taken over thirty years to reduce our nation to moral degeneracy, national impotence, and economic inflation. If Christians and other pro-moralists worked together, we could return it to moral sanity in ten to fifteen years."[21] This, in LaHaye's view, is both the Christian and the American thing to do. He notes that Dante reserved the hottest places in Hell for "those who, in times of moral crises, maintain their neutrality." Such passivity in the face of a deadly threat is precisely why the humanist menace has been allowed to grow to such alarming proportions.

When the Committee for the Survival of a Free Congress becomes involved, the imagery grows even more obviously militaristic and the call to battle is even more specific. CSFC is a Washington-based, nonpartisan corporation founded by Paul Weyrich, and supports various conservative causes, particularly those that bear upon legislative decisions in the U.S. Congress. The committee doesn't hesitate to meet issues head on, especially vigorously when they involve the subject of religion.

Under CSFC's sponsorship, William H. Marshner, professor of theology at Christendom College in Front Royal, Virginia, has prepared a document, "The New Creatures and the New Politics," which provides counsel to Christians on how to conduct themselves in the crisis at hand. According to Marshner, America has become the modern Sodom, as evidenced by the ease with which secular humanist values have risen to ascendancy in the culture. Marshner lists the familiar problems: sex education in the schools, values-clarification courses, behaviorism, communes, the legacy of Haight-Ashbury, and so on. Such examples of moral deterioration make it easier for communism to take over the country and the world, the potential outcome of the dilemma in which Western culture finds itself.

It bothers Marshner that Christians from the left, such as Daniel Berrigan and Martin Luther King, Jr., are able to engage in political activity and no one questions their involvement; but when Christians from the right become politically active, they are charged with violations of the separation of church and state. Marshner wants to correct this and to fit rightist Christians for effective political action. He recognizes that some of his readers will object that the Christian task is to convert people to Christ, not to remove liberals from power, but responds: "Sorry, I don't see the incompatibility. A liberal out of power is more likely to repent at leisure. Besides, these days, getting liberals out of power is a directly Christian goal in its own right; it is the only way to protect their victims from any further doses of the liberal policies." Then Marshner gets down to specifics:

> Finally, and speaking directly to the issue of saving the souls of the liberals themselves, I am firmly convinced that removing them from power is the first prerequisite.
> What happens to such a person when his own ideology is rejected at the polls? . . .
> His convictions are shattered, his tin god is broken; he becomes open to Christian truth for perhaps the first time in his life. So let's help him out. Let's love this particular enemy by making him obsolescent.[22]

In all such portrayals of the present drama, military terminology is employed to describe the conflict between two diametrically opposed forces: one right, the other wrong; one of truth, the other of error; one benevolent, the other malevolent; one of freedom, the other of bondage; one godly, the other godless. Whenever it is mentioned within this context, the Vietnam War stands as a graphic illustration of enervated resolve resulting from the diabolical, unchecked humanist-socialist-Communist conspiracy. Francis A. Schaeffer, to whom Falwell, LaHaye, and others look for intellectual guidance, describes it this way: "It is not too strong to say that we are at war, and there are no neutral parties in the struggle. One either confesses that God is the final authority, or one confesses that Caesar is Lord."[23]

As indicated, the Vietnam War is an important component of the mythological drama that advocates of the new religious right envision as unfolding. By definition–in terms that Falwell, LaHaye, Schaeffer, Weyrich, and the others make quite precise–the Vietnam War is unfinished; it was never brought to satisfactory conclusion, and its elements are continuing. The dramatic confrontation cannot be restricted to the particular circumstances of open military battle–say, from the Gulf of Tonkin Resolution to the return of troops in 1975. Instead, the Vietnam War is a symbol of the perennial battle, containing almost all of the principal ingredients of the enduring warfare between truth and error, right and wrong, eternal life and unending death.

What the Vietnam War pointed up most alarmingly of all was the deficiency of American resolve. The U.S. loss can be utilized to unmask the collective moral decay of the country, and when such attempts are made, the causal lines point to the influence of alien, secular philosophy. If America had stayed faithful to the principles upon which the nation was founded, the outcome of the war would doubtless have been different. Indeed, through American intransigence and moral ineptitude, the war served to put the nation more deeply into the hole. The same happens whenever the principles of the founding fathers are accorded second place to those of socialists and secular humanists. Therefore, the Vietnam War stands as a beacon of what can happen when American resolve is conflicted and true and false conceptions of American destiny are pitted against one another. Unless those who wish to return the country to the principles upon which it was founded find ways to be successful, the same will happen on a larger scale.

In theological terms, the issue concerns the power of the covenant. Though Jerry Falwell, the Moral Majority, and their adherents will not equate the United States of America with the kingdom of God, they are quite willing to grant America a favored-nation status – not, they point out, because of anything Americans have earned, but because of the beneficence of the Almighty. The United States can maintain the blessing of God if it keeps certain covenantal conditions, such as Falwell's favorite, from Genesis 12:3: "Those that bless you I will bless, and those that curse you, I will execrate." The most reprehensible deed is to doubt, question, or reject the assumption that the United States of America has been granted this status and destiny.

In terms of the Vietnam War, Americans committed the gross sins of lack of confidence and failure of courage, both at home and abroad. To respond this way was to dishonor the covenant, and its attendant blessings, which resides at the heart of the religiously sanctioned *idea of America*. If Americans had been true to the covenant, the war could have proceeded to successful resolution, and a portion of the opponent's relentless drive toward world domination could have been halted, stemmed, or reversed. Now, following the tragedy, the ground is much more difficult to make up. The good news, however, is that the outcome of the war shocked the guardians of the fundamental covenant from apathy into action; hence the rise of the new religious and political right and the equipping of fundamentalist Christianity with clear and resolute political intentions. Americans are now resolving that the outcome of all subsequent skirmishes in which battle lines are drawn in the same way will follow the dictates of the covenant.

This is the reason, as George McGovern and others have noted with considerable dismay, that the New Right has captured the prominent positive national symbols: nationalistic feeling, patriotism, the family, motherhood, virtue, and moral rectitude. It is the reason that advocates of the new religious right feel proud to wear the American flag in their lapels or on tieclasps (never mind that they are also wearing "Jesus First" pins), and that many are supporting the current remilitarization of the country – the development of missile systems, increased military spending, and a much more aggressive military rhetoric.

The alternative is not always easy to enunciate. After all, it was Lyndon Baines Johnson, the liberal architect of the Great Society, who defended the U.S. presence in Vietnam by stating that America remains "humankind's best hope." It was the liberal John Fitzgerald Kennedy who looked to Vietnam as fit soil on which to establish the American free-enterprise system. Who within the nation can mount a counterargument without appearing to be soft on communism or allowing that it might be acceptable to become number two?

The liberal alternative involves a careful reexamination of the objectives of the Great Society in light of its successes and failures and of current senses of the nation's fundamental needs. Such reconstructive analyses and proposals as those of Senator Paul Tsongas in his book *The Road from Here: Liberalism and Realities in the 1980s* and the guidelines marked out by the President's [Carter's] Commission for a National Agenda for the Eighties, a summary of which is contained in a volume entitled *A National Agenda for the Eighties,* are most useful. In the same category are a new periodical, *democracy,* edited by Sheldon Wolin, the proposed agenda of George McGovern's Americans for Common Sense, and other publications and political interest groups which have come into being since Ronald Reagan was elected in 1980. Because the challenges are large and the responses (both theoretical and programmatic) must be meticulous and sure, however, efforts of this kind attract less immediate attention than those that translate more readily into an Armageddon mind-set. The task liberals face is awesome: to respond to Armageddon with something other than adversarial vengeance, without sounding like voices emanating from some idyllic cosmic Eden.

There is realism in Arthur Schlesinger's observation that

there's a very great sense of frustration overhanging, left from the Vietnam War. I'm not so sure it's all been turned inward. When one remembers the debate over the Panama Canal treaties, for example, clearly a lot of rage which that debate generated sprang from the fact that a lot of Americans felt, well, maybe we couldn't lick the Vietnamese, but we still have the Panamanians to kick around. And I think that some of the frustrations that have taken place earlier . . . on the questions of Iran, or Mexico, or Afghanistan, or Ethiopia, stem from that feeling—that somehow we must find we are powerful, and we're wonderful, and we're filled with virtue, and we must find ways of making our virtue and our power more effective in the world. Whereas it would seem to me that the lesson of Vietnam is that our motives aren't all that different from those of any other country, and that there are limits to our power and our virtue, and that we're not omnipotent and we're not omniscient, and that we must, instead of trying to run the whole world, we must try to define where our vital interests lie and concentrate our power and concern there.[24]

And yet even to talk this way—albeit in positive revisionist terms—is to confirm that the American spirit has been profoundly chastened.

8. The Healing Process

"I regard the war in Indochina as the greatest military, political, economic, and moral blunder in our national history."

— GEORGE MCGOVERN

"Unless the United States shakes the false lessons of Vietnam and puts the 'Vietnam syndrome' behind it, we will forfeit the security of our allies and eventually our own. This is the real lesson of Vietnam—not that we should abandon power, but that unless we learn to use it effectively to defend our interests, the tables of history will be turned against us and all we believe in."

— RICHARD NIXON

"The era of self-doubt is over."
— RONALD REAGAN
(Commencement Address, U.S. Military Academy, West Point, May 27, 1981)

AS WE HAVE SEEN, a primary characteristic of the Armageddon mentality is the eagerness to divide the world into sharp contrasts: right versus wrong, truth versus error, good versus evil, light versus dark, providence versus waywardness, blessings versus curses, in the most rigorous fashion possible. The mechanism that enforces this way of thought is the fusion of the contrast between America and anti-America with a revised Manichaean mythology about the fundamental and pervasive conflict between God and the Devil.

The world of Armageddon is shaped by conflict. The forces that prevail in life are the ones that win, that defeat their foes and demonstrate their superiority on the battlefield. Confrontations make allegiances firm, choices irreconcilable, and fidelities absolute. Events are always decisive, and the colossal drama toward which all things point is final. In Armageddon, the destiny of the world is enacted in struggles to the finish between diametrically opposed power centers.

Eden resonates differently. Whatever boundaries pertain only differentiate Eden from all else; they have no internal bearing. Everything in Eden belongs; all inhabitants are citizens, and all are entitled to the resources of Eden, without exception. There are no hierarchies, no polarization, no stratification, no class struggle. There are no decisive choices, either; the goal is simply to maintain Eden. Eden is garden instead of battleground, it is harmony rather than conflict. It is warm, fecund, full of vegetation, beautiful, alluring, original, and all-encompassing. But Eden lacks precision.

The radical differences between the expectations of Armageddon and the impulses of Eden provide the framework for much of what has happened within the United States, and throughout the world, in the post–World War II era. Some of the time, for some of the people, motivation has come from Armageddon, while for others the compulsions have been those of Eden. The one encourages a readiness to confront the adversary; its temper is tough, resolute, defensive, self-protective. The other exhibits an interest in enunciating the underlying harmony; it speaks of maintaining the essential components of the living environment while proclaiming the blessings of global harmony.

The two agendas, therefore, differ markedly. The basic distinction is, in Irving Kristol's words, between "the patriotic temper, the politics of national assertion," and the "social democratic temper, the inward-looking politics of compassionate reform."[1] Both have been present in the American collective consciousness from the beginning, and for long periods there was balance between them. For most of the post–World War II era, however, the inhabitants of Eden and the advocates of Armageddon have been at such severe odds that it has been as if there were two United States of America, competing with each other for supremacy and the allegiance of the citizenry.

Within the counterculture, the Eden mentality found ascendancy, while during the following period, a time of counter-revolution, the mood of national assertiveness reemerged. The trauma of Vietnam was a product of the projection of this fundamental quarrel onto the battlefield; what became most visible during the war was America in conflict with America — the dark night within the nation's soul. The war remains unfinished because the quarrel has not been resolved.

How did it happen this way? What forces gave the drama such orientation?

Dean Acheson, secretary of state under President Truman, offered some reminiscences that illuminate these questions. Writing in a book appropriately titled *Present at the Creation,* Acheson stated that it took some while for Americans to recognize that "the whole world structure and order that we had inherited from the nineteenth century was gone" after World War II. What replaced it, Acheson observed, was a struggle "directed from two bitterly opposed and ideologically irreconcilable power centers"[2] — the world's great superpowers, whose rivalry had a pervasive influence upon all significant subsequent events.

Nearly thirty years later, Richard Nixon described the fundamental challenge in almost the same language that Acheson had used:

> The old colonial empires are gone. The new Soviet imperialism requires a new counterforce to keep it in check. The United States cannot provide this alone, but without strong and effective leadership from the United States, it cannot be provided at all. We cannot afford to waffle and waver. Either we act like a great power or we will be reduced to a minor power, and thus reduced we will not survive — nor will freedom or Western values survive.[3]

The United States certainly wished to have it both ways: to retain some semblance of the world structure that it inherited from the nineteenth century (enough, that is to say, to support strong alliances between former colonial powers, the majority of which continued to identify themselves as allies within the "free world"), and at the same time, to make certain that the contest with the Soviet Union would be played out in its favor.

As it happened, the beginning of strong United States involvement in Vietnam coincides exactly with the beginning of the construction of this postwar U.S. foreign policy. Similarly, the period in which the United States' presence was felt in Vietnam – from September 2, 1945, to May 1, 1975 – coincides exactly with the period in which these foreign-policy objectives were being enunciated. Thus it was to be expected that American policy toward Vietnam would reflect the tension between these two competing principles.

From Harry Truman to Gerald Ford, all framers of American foreign policy had to act as if the principles were compatible in order to speak in clear and resolute terms about America's interests in Vietnam. Each said that the United States was in Southeast Asia because of its deep desire to maintain a benevolent and workable world structure. Each explained that the extension of American power and influence into Southeast Asia had been encouraged by humanitarian concerns. Each defended American involvement on the grounds that it had been requested by people seeking emancipation from oppression, saying that people wishing to take their place among the strong and self-reliant nations of the modern world had sought the counsel and assistance of the world's leader. All these expressed motives were in full keeping with the legacy of images that had been utilized across the centuries to describe what America stands for. That same legacy could be tapped to show that American involvement in Vietnam corresponded to the best within the national character.

It took but a short additional step for John F. Kennedy to look to Vietnam as the potential testing ground in Southeast Asia for the heretofore remarkably successful American-styled democratic system.[4] Lyndon Johnson merely followed the sequence, adding his own particularities, when he spoke with enthusiasm about making the Mekong Delta as resourceful as the valley of the Tennessee River. Naturally Johnson also looked ahead to the time that the goals of the Great Society would be transmitted to Indochina, after the local skirmishes there had been brought to resolution.

As such high hopes and confidences were repeated, the American leadership provided assurances that our motives were pure. "We seek no territory for ourselves," Johnson reiterated. Ostensibly, America had not become active in Vietnam to promote selfish ambitions, to advance its own desires, or even to protect its vested interests. All that it attempted could be justified on the basis of the cardinal principle – the need to maintain a stable and benevolent world order.

Unfortunately, this professed altruistic motive became hopelessly entangled with the discordant twin objective of winning the competition with the rival power center. Before long, it became inevitable that the second objective would be taken as the means to insure the realization of the first. An expectation grew that stable world order could be achieved if the United States could win the contest with the Soviet Union, now simply referred to as the adversary. Logically speaking, the two principles were interdependent from the very moment following the end of the Second World War when foreign policy was being reformulated.

By the time that John F. Kennedy gave his Inaugural Address on January 20, 1961, each of the two principles could be expressed in the words of the other: "Let every nation know, whether it wishes us well or ill, that we shall pay any price, bear any burden, meet any hardship, support any friend, oppose any foe, in order to assure the survival and the success of liberty." This was a large promise, to be made good within the intrinsic conflicts of those postwar realignments that had been set in motion even as Ho Chi Minh was declaring Vietnamese independence.

Accordingly, when crucial choices were placed before American decision-makers, the outcome was inevitable. Certainly most U.S. Presidents wished to have it both ways – to keep the two objectives in harmony and balance. When they couldn't, however – when the twin ambitions became manifestly incompatible and contradictory – the leaders found most support in advancing the American cause against its primary competition. No American President could afford politically to be soft on communism, so each felt obliged to push the get-tough policy to prominence. In doing so, each allowed the ideological struggle to assume critical and strategic dominance, and whenever this occurred, the "patriotic temper" (promoting "the politics of national assertion") gained mastery over the "inward-looking politics of compassionate reform." The same temper won out in the leaders' attitude toward the nation's involvement in Vietnam: Vietnam was the testing ground not simply for the free-enterprise system, but for the conflict in American will and resolve, manifested for the entire world, including the American citizenry.

If the United States had not invested the situation in Vietnam with rivalry with Communist powers, the tragedy might have been avoided. If it had perceived the conflict as a civil war, it would have had no good reason to become involved. If it had seen the situation simply as a clash between colonialists and nationalists, it might not have entered military engagement. But because it viewed the war as part of the fundamental conflict between the world's two great superpowers, the United States eventually felt a responsibility to commit its forces. The quality and intensity of that commitment was nurtured by the religious sanctions of the patriotic temper and the Manichaean mythology by which the rivalry was expressed. In this rendition, America was placed on the side of good, in opposition to evil. Light was pitted against darkness, freedom against bondage, America against anti-America – yes, even God against the Devil.

Within a relatively brief span of time, therefore, the postwar world became sharply polarized, exhibiting all of the characteristic invitations for takeover by an Armageddon mentality. By the time of the Gulf of Tonkin Resolution in 1964, the way had been cleared by Korea in 1950, the Berlin blockade in 1961, and the Cuban missile crisis in 1963. All of these challenges had been met successfully, to America's advantage. Vietnam was simply next in the series. The nation could be confident that the problem would be solved in a relatively short time. But by now the equations were inexact.

To be sure, Ho Chi Minh espoused the Communist philosophy and had strong loyalties to both China and the Soviet Union. He had been trained in the teachings of Marx and Lenin and was thoroughly committed to Marxist thought and the Communist social and political program. Yet the plot the Americans envisioned bore only generalized application to the actual drama in Vietnam. U.S. leadership tried to direct the scenes with little or no knowledge of local circumstances and incentives. It tried to erect in South Vietnam a government which the people clearly resisted. It wished to promote certain Western forms of democratic decision-making among a people who had had no preparation and had shown no strong inclinations for them. It possessed only slight acquaintance with the indigenous sociocultural matrix, based on a combination of Confucian, Taoist, Buddhist, and native religious influences and organized according to ancient Chinese mandarinic systems. It was as if the plot had been written by someone who had not yet visited the territory and had been imposed much more because of the plight of the outsiders than because it concerned the affairs of the Vietnamese.

Stanley Hoffmann, a Harvard specialist in international government, describes American military and political hubris in Vietnam this way:

> The central problem of American policy—of any policy—is the relevance of its ends to specific cases: the more ambitious or ideological a policy, the more indispensable it is to analyze the realities of each case with critical rigor before applying to it one's concepts or preconceptions, for otherwise the statesmen will trip into the pitfalls of irrelevance, "adventurism," or unreality.

He continues:

> Our own policy was of necessity ambitious because of our very role as a superpower; and it has, if not an ideology, at least a set of principles and dogmas such as resistance to aggression, attachment to self-

determination, opposition to forceful communist
takeovers, etc. . . .
*The tragedy of our course in Vietnam lies in our refusal
to come to grips with those realities in South Vietnam that
happened to be decisive from the viewpoint of politics.*[5]

Understandably, all such ventures are doomed to failure
because they embody the expectation that the structure and
order of the world can be established and maintained if the
United States achieves success in its contest with its chief rival.

Beguiled and misshaped by the full weight of the mythological anticipation – that it was a righteous cause and that
righteousness should prevail – the military venture was
confutable from the first. Because it was under the same
banner of miscarried intentions that the crusaders fought, the
wounded warriors returned from the hostilities having both
lost and failed; and no one is able clearly to discern which is
which. Both outcomes contradict the expectations in the prevailing mythology. Indeed, they challenge the reliability of the
mythology directly. The successful and heroic exploits of the
combatants can hardly be celebrated – even the most highly
decorated veterans of the war remain virtually unknown to the
American public – because no one knows clearly what success
could ever mean. So the soldiers return, having lost and having
failed, and find no lasting reconciliation. Looking back, they
are still not sure what it was they were in Vietnam to do.

Certainly Vietnam was war, but it was also theater, viewed
around the world, and thus encouraged discordant American
motives to become visible. Such motives were assigned to
characters, many of whom tried to express their opposition to
the script. Disclosing aspects of the American soul that circumstances had never made perceptible before, the play was inevitably a tragedy, though it was enacted through collective
psychic melodrama. Thus Vietnam was a war made visible in a
variety of theaters, and it was theater that made the dynamics
of warfare self-conscious.

Humankind had never before been able to penetrate the
nature of war from such close range, so the trauma was not

simply something to which people formed a response. Instead, it embodied the self-consciousness within which the warfare was occurring. The play was about ideology, about America, about coming of age. Most of all, it addressed the consequences of the loss of innocence.

In his masterful book *The American Adam*, R. W. B. Lewis explores the variety of ways in which the imagery of the New World is treated in American literature. The discovery of America as the occasion for a new Adam and a second chance for humanity has been treated by Hawthorne, Melville, Whitman, Browne, Emerson, and Thoreau as well as by more contemporary writers such as Faulkner, Salinger, and Bellow. Central to their imagery, according to Lewis, is the quest for innocence, which makes claims on a renewed or recaptured innocence, as this has been expressed through a recurrent revitalization of Adam traditions throughout American literature.[6]

The Vietnam War is about innocence too, not the quest for innocence, but the loss of American innocence. Through it the imagery of the restorative and re-creative power of the New World – Lyndon Johnson's "last best hope for mankind" – was plunged again and again into what Lewis calls "the spurious disruptive rituals of the actual world." After this experience, assumptions of innocence could never be the same again. No clear-eyed, wide-open sense that as Americans, we are here to make the world a better place. No vigorous sense of trust and confidence. No Billy Budd. No opportunity for undiminished heroism. No new or recent esteemed warriors. No John Wayne. No Joe DiMaggio. Only the sounds, the confusion, the self-doubt and self-hate, and the need to get back on track after our efforts to come to grips with the realities of the thermonuclear age.

Jerry Falwell knows the feeling. In talking about the need to return to the principles of the nation's founding fathers, he really wishes to reestablish the conditions that will make the vanishing dream come to life again. In many respects, the un-resolved character of the Vietnam War created Jerry Falwell and influenced the message his support groups send out. Similarly, the contemplatives and spiritualists recognize that they must find, or perhaps re-create, the dream from within, since again, borrowing Lewis's phrasing, "they can scarcely locate it any longer in the historic world about them."[7] All are responding in predictable ways to the same set of conditions.

Ronald Reagan knows the feeling, too. During his first months as President, for example, he spoke to reporters about patriotism, heroism, devotion to country, national pride, and the perennial collective virtues. He told them he wished U.S. citizens could sustain the unifying spirit they had experienced during the return of the hostages from Iran. Then, citing a scene from a silent western movie he had seen "back when I was a boy," the President told the story of an outlaw who wanted to rob a mail train; the outlaw was dissuaded from doing so by a companion, who said, "Look, the bank is all right, the stagecoach too, but you don't monkey around with Uncle Sam." Pleased with the story, the President asked the reporters, "How long has it been since anyone felt that way about our national government – that, by golly, you don't futz around with Uncle Sam?"[8]

The President exhibited the same get-tough stance at his first news conference in February 1981, when stating that he knew of "no leader of the Soviet Union since the Revolution who did not pursue the goal of world revolution." He elaborated by suggesting that "the only morality they recognize is what will further their cause, meaning they reserve unto themselves the right to commit any crime, to lie, to cheat."[9]

The next month, at a special White House ceremony for Roy Benavidez, a forty-five-year-old retired Army sergeant presented with a Medal of Honor for bravery in Vietnam, Reagan struck the same tone. Alluding to the recent enthusiastic and tumultuous welcome the nation had given the returning hostages, the President lamented the situation of Vietnam War veterans. When they had returned, he said, "they were greeted by no parades, no bands, no waving of the flag they so nobly served." He explained that "they came home without victory because they had been denied permission to win." Then, drawing the lesson, he declared: "Never again do we send an active fighting force to a country unless it is for a cause we intend to win."[10]

At the same time, in the first months of his term, Reagan's staff was preparing legislation authorizing a monumental increase in military spending. There was much talk about the new resolve of the nation to do whatever was necessary to remedy any situation that found America in a number-two position. The words "our adversary," deliberately unused during the Carter years, became prominent again in official Washington's vocabulary. It goes without saying that no one needed to ask just who "our adversary" was.

Thus, barely six years after the war in Vietnam had been brought to a painful and unsatisfying end, most of the fundamental ideological and symbolic preconditions that had brought it into being were back again. Cold War rhetoric had intensified; adversarial postures had been resumed; bipolar tensions had returned. In addition there was renewed eagerness to interpret events as directed or influenced, as Dean Acheson said, "from two bitterly opposed and ideologically irreconcilable power centers."

Hedrick Smith is not alone in believing that Ronald Reagan's world is "a throwback to the 1950s when American power was paramount." Smith calls it "the bipolar world of the early Cold War," and comments that "the global power rivalry with Moscow not only animates [Reagan's] thinking about foreign affairs" but is also "the prism through which he views the entire world." Smith finds the President to be "ill at ease" with "diffusion of power," so that upon assuming office he set out to reverse the American decline.[11]

Reagan's attitudes are in keeping with Richard Nixon's recommendations as to how the United States should conduct itself in the post-Vietnam era. Nixon wrote:

> Having dealt directly and at great length with the Soviet Union, I know that they exploit weakness but respect strength If they see a new strength in the

American sinew, a new firmness in the American step, a new steel in the American eye, then two things will happen. They will be more cautious in their adventuring, and they will also be more realistic in their negotiating. If they think they can roll us, they will try to roll us. If they conclude that they have to deal with us, they will try to deal with us.[12]

Is it that the trauma of Vietnam has already been erased from memory, that many have already "shaken it," in Nixon's words? Or is it that the seething frustrations of the war gave rise to powerful and explosive resentments? For whatever reasons, all of the necessary preconditions for such conflict had returned by the early 1980s, when the Armageddon connection was stronger, more direct, and more explicit than ever before. It elevated the rivalry between the two irreconcilable power centers to a mythological status, and this time the opposition between the superpowers was being equated in clear terms with the cataclysmic clash between good and evil and their concomitants.

The President looked to the Scriptures to support this view; on more than one occasion he expressed: "I have long believed there was a divine plan that placed this land here to be found by a people of a special kind, that we have a rendezvous with destiny."[13] He also seemed to be in league with the prophets of Armageddon, consulting with Dr. Falwell about administrative appointments, appearing at a meeting of the Religious Roundtable in Dallas in August 1980, where he assured the evangelical preachers of his support of their cause, and promising at conservative Bob Jones University that if elected, he would work to overturn the IRS rule prohibiting segregated private colleges from tax-exempt status. President Reagan appeared with Falwell before students on the campus of Liberty Baptist College in Lynchburg; he appointed his religious liaison officer during the campaign, Robert Billings, as assistant secretary of education (Billings's son, William, is executive director of the National Christian Action Coalition). The President's essay on "What July Fourth Means to Me" in the commemorative June 28, 1981, issue of *Parade* appeared to follow, in both outline and content, Falwell's treatment of the subject of freedom in *Listen America!*[14] Much of the President's rhetoric was taken from the vocabulary of Armageddon, and the new administration tended to approach each of the world's potential crises as occasions to achieve the competitive edge over the Communists. On the global scale, the administration approached the nations of lesser power according to the same mythology, as satellites of either Michael and his angels or the Devil and his legions.

As this tendency was growing and strengthening, the veterans of Vietnam were quietly finding their way back into American society. Still carrying the heaviest burdens of the war, some – not all – were experiencing grave difficulty. They had become symbols of the nation's shame, unwelcome reminders of collective uncertainty and potential scapegoats of the desire to make amends. It would not satisfy them to be told that war is war, combat is combat, a soldier is a soldier. In the new interpretations, blame for the war was being shifted from those who instigated it to those who opposed it, and the veterans found themselves included in still another controversy about Vietnam.

In addition, their experience in the war enabled the veterans to look deeply into the American soul, where they witnessed the conflict, encountered the ambivalence, and were pulled by discordant motivations. They were direct participants in the disruptive ritual act that spelled loss of American innocence, and thus it is not surprising that it is from their pens and from their first-person mode of communication that the story is being told.

It is a story of killing and infanticide along both sides of the battle lines. The landscape has been despoiled; millions of people have been left homeless. Premeditated acts of murder have occurred, and hands are still stained with blood. This record of the combatants' involvement is there for the entire world to see and judge.

Tom Bird, a former U.S. infantryman who was captured in North Vietnam and held in prison until the war ended, was among the group of four American veterans who returned to Hanoi shortly before Christmas 1981. Describing a part of what happened, Bird explained: "The other day I told some Vietnamese officials in Hanoi that I killed some of their people. I needed to tell them. They said they understood." He added, "With this, the war finally stopped in my mind."[15]

Similar acts of confession are taking place daily in the centers of the Veterans Outreach Program which have been established throughout the country. Such centers have become sanctuaries wherein veterans experience the necessary ritual healing, and where confession is the pathway leading to re-socialization and the resumption of an active place in American life. Though they would surely make no specific claim to be serving in such a capacity, the counselors in these centers and in the streets are doing the work of confessors, serving as unordained priests. Furthermore, in more communities than most people realize the vet centers have come to assume some of the roles of neighborhood religious communities, where everyone is devoted to allowing the healing process to follow its own course.

The collective healing process must follow a similar course. The largest question of all is whether this process will be encouraged or whether it will be interrupted or canceled by either utopian aspirations or cataclysmic expectations. A world so easily divisible into such absolute contrasts is already severely fragmented. The real issue is whether healing can occur and wholeness be discovered before the trauma of the unfinished war is reenacted.

Notes

Chapter 1

1. *Los Angeles Times*, Wednesday, September 16, 1981, part VI, pp. 1 and 8.
2. *Los Angeles Times*, Wednesday, September 16, 1981, part II, pp. 1 and 3.
3. David Christian, "A Vietnam Hero Finds the Real War Is on the Home Front," *People*, September 14, 1981, pp. 49-50.
4. Phil McCombs, "At Vietnam Reunion, Not-So-Friendly Fire," *Washington Post*, November 21, 1981, p. A2.
5. "Veterans Lay War to Rest in Vietnam," *Los Angeles Times*, December 26, 1981, part II, p. 2.
6. *Los Angeles Times*, December 29, 1981, part I, p. 18.
7. This was a special survey conducted by Research and Forecasts, Inc., commissioned by Connecticut Mutual Life Insurance Company, and distributed in pamphlet form by Connecticut Mutual.
8. George Gallup, Jr., and David Poling, *The Search for America's Faith* (Nashville: Abingdon, 1980).
9. T. George Harris, "Introduction: Spiritual Terror in the Ecstatic Eighties," in Jeffrey K. Hadden and Charles E. Swann, *Prime-Time Preachers: The Rising Power of Televangelism* (Reading, Mass.: Addison-Wesley, 1981), pp. xix-xx.
10. Morris Dickstein, *Gates of Eden: American Culture in the Sixties* (New York: Basic Books, 1977), p. 271.
11. Ibid., p. 261.

Chapter 2

1. Ho Chi Minh, "Speech at the Tours Congress," in *Ho Chi Minh: Selected Writings, 1920–1969* (Hanoi: Foreign Languages Publishing House, 1973), pp. 16-17.
2. Ho Chi Minh, "Report on the National and Colonial Questions at the Fifth Congress of the Communist International," in *Selected Writings*, pp. 31-32.
3. Ibid., p. 36.
4. Ho Chi Minh, "Appeal Made on the Occasion of the Founding of the Indochinese Communist Party (February 18, 1930)," in *Selected Writings*, pp. 39-40.
5. Ibid., p. 40.

6. Ibid., p. 41
7. Ho Chi Minh, "Letter from Abroad," in *Selected Writings*, pp. 44-46.
8. Ho Chi Minh, "Declaration of Independence of the Democratic Republic of Viet Nam," in *Selected Writings*, p. 53.
9. Ibid., p. 55.
10. Ho Chi Minh, "To Our Fellow-Countrymen in Nam Bo Before Going to France for Negotiations," in *Selected Writings*, p. 66.
11. Ho Chi Minh, "Appeal for Nation-Wide Resistance," in *Selected Writings*, p. 68.

Chapter 3

1. "Policy and Information Statement on Indochina," July 1947, Philippine and Southeast Asia Branch File, U.S. Department of State Records, Box 10.
2. George C. Marshall, Statement of United States Embassy in Paris, February 3, 1947, recorded in *Foreign Relations of the United States*, 1947, VI, pp. 67-68.
3. Dean Acheson, *Present at the Creation: My Years in the State Department* (New York: W. W. Norton, 1969), pp. 670-71.
4. Dwight D. Eisenhower, *Mandate for Change* (New York: Doubleday, 1963), p. 336.
5. Ho Chi Minh, "Answers to the Press on U.S. Intervention in Indochina (July 25, 1950), " in *Selected Writings*, p. 95.
6. Ho Chi Minh, "On the Fifth Anniversary of the August Revolution and National Day," in *Selected Writings*, pp. 96-97.
7. Eisenhower, *Mandate for Change*, pp. 374-75.
8. John F. Kennedy, *The Strategy of Peace* (New York: Harper and Row, 1960), p. 61.
9. Allan Nevins, ed., in Kennedy, *The Strategy of Peace*, p. 62n.
10. *New York Times*, Wednesday, August 5, 1964, p. A1.
11. Thomas J. Hamilton, "Stevenson Says Goal Is to Keep Southeast Asia Independent," *New York Times*, Thursday, August 6, 1964, p. A1.
12. *New York Times*, August 6, 1964, p. A2.
13. Marvin E. Gettleman, ed., *Vietnam: History, Documents, and Opinions on a Major World Crisis* (New York: Fawcett, 1965), pp. 382-385, passim.
14. *New York Times*, August 8, 1964, p. A1.
15. Robert Jay Lifton, *Boundaries: Psychological Man in Revolution* (New York: Random House, 1970), p. 43.

Chapter 4

1. Gettleman, *Vietnam*, pp. 386-87.
2. Lyndon B. Johnson, "A Pattern for Peace in Southeast Asia (the Johns

Hopkins Speech, April 7, 1965)," in *Department of State Bulletin*, LII (April 26, 1965), pp. 606-10.

3. U.S. Department of State, "Aggression from the North: The Record of North Viet-Nam's Campaign to Conquer South Viet-Nam," Far Eastern Series 130 (February 1965), frontispiece, pp. 1-64, passim.

4. Ho Chi Minh, "Address to the Second Session of the Third National Assembly of the Democratic Republic of Vietnam" (April 10, 1965), in *Selected Writings*, p. 298.

5. Lyndon Baines Johnson, *The Vantage Point: Perspectives of the Presidency, 1963–1969* (New York: Holt, Rinehart and Winston, 1971), p. 249.

6. Ibid.

7. Ibid.

8. Ibid., pp. 437-38.

9. Henry Kissinger, *White House Years* (Boston: Little, Brown, 1979), pp. 57-58, 61.

10. Arthur Schlesinger, Jr., "The Roots of Misconceptions," in Richard M. Pfeffer, ed., *No More Vietnams? The War and the Future of American Foreign Policy* (New York: Harper and Row, 1968), pp. 8, 9.

11. James C. Thomson, "The Lessons of Vietnam," in Pfeffer, *No More Vietnams?*, p. 288.

12. Robert B. Semple, Jr., *New York Times*, May 1, 1970, p. A1.

13. Kissinger, *White House Years*, pp. 485-86.

14. Louis A. Fanning, *Betrayal in Vietnam* (New Rochelle: Arlington, 1976), Appendix B, pp. 241-44.

15. Ibid., pp. 245-47.

16. W. Scott Thompson and Donaldson D. Frizzell, eds., *The Lessons of Vietnam* (New York: Crane, Russak, 1977), pp. iii-iv.

Chapter 5

1. Michael Herr, *Dispatches* (New York: Knopf, 1968), p. 45.

2. Frances FitzGerald, *Fire in the Lake: The Vietnamese and the Americans in Vietnam* (Boston: Atlantic/Little, Brown, 1972), p. 14.

3. Philip Caputo, *A Rumor of War* (New York: Holt, Rinehart and Winston, 1977), pp. 5-6, 4, xv.

4. Gloria Emerson, *Winners and Losers: Battles, Retreats, Gains, Losses and Ruins from the Vietnam War* (New York: Harcourt Brace Jovanovich, 1976), p. 20.

5. Ibid., p. 25-26.

6. Al Santoli, *Everything We Had: An Oral History of the Vietnam War by Thirty-Three American Soldiers Who Fought It* (New York: Random House, 1981), p. 63.

7. Ibid., p. 47.

8. Personal testimony.

9. Santoli, *Everything We Had*, p. 48.

10. Personal testimony.
11. Personal testimony.
12. Santoli, *Everything We Had*, p. 55.
13. Frederick Downs, *The Killing Zone: My Life in the Vietnam War* (New York: W. W. Norton, 1978), p. 11.
14. Personal testimony.
15. William Jayne, "Immigrants from the Combat Zone," in A. D. Horne, *The Wounded Generation: America After Vietnam* (Englewood Cliffs, N.J.: Prentice-Hall, 1981), p. 161.
16. Lawrence M. Baskir and William A. Strauss, *Chance and Circumstance: The Draft, the War and the Vietnam Generation* (New York: Random House, 1978), p. 251.
17. Ibid., pp. 254-55.
18. Peter Tauber, *The Last Best Hope* (New York: Harcourt Brace Jovanovich, 1977), pp. 26-27.
19. Santoli, *Everything We Had*, pp. 177-78.
20. Ibid., p. 249.
21. Ibid., p. 109.
22. Emerson, *Winners and Losers*, p. 372.
23. Ibid., p. 374.
24. Personal testimony.
25. Clifford Geertz, "Religion as a Cultural System," in Michael Banton, ed., *Anthropological Approaches to the Study of Religion* (London: Tavistock, 1966), pp. 1-46, passim.
26. Herr, *Dispatches*, p. 65.
27. Ibid., pp. 56-57.
28. Baskir and Strauss, *Chance and Circumstance*, p. 13.
29. Ibid., p. 6.
30. David Halberstam, *The Best and the Brightest* (New York: Random House, 1969), pp. 806-807.
31. Herr, *Dispatches*, p. 41.
32. Santoli, *Everything We Had*, p. 5.

Chapter 6

1. This thesis is explored in the author's article, "The Vietnam War and American Values," *The Center Magazine* XI, no. 4, pp. 18-26, portions of which are included in this chapter.
2. Ron Rosenbaum, "The Subterranean World of the Bomb," *Harper's* March, 1978), pp. 88-89.
3. Dickstein, *Gates of Eden*, pp. 40, ix, 271.
4. Ivan Morris, *The Nobility of Failure: Tragic Heroes in the History of Japan* (New York: Holt, Rinehart and Winston, 1975), pp. 38-39.

5. Quoted in William Theodore de Bary, ed., *The Buddhist Tradition in India, China and Japan* (New York: Random House, 1972), p. 97.

6. Alan Watts, *In My Own Way* (New York: Random House, 1973), pp. 442-43.

7. Allen Ginsberg, "The Change: Kyoto-Tokyo Express, July 18, 1963," *The New Writing in the U.S.A.*, Donald Allen and Robert Creeley, eds. (Middlesex, England: Harmond, England, 1967), p. 89.

8. Colin Wilson, *The Outsider* (London: Gollancz, 1956).

Chapter 7

1. Dickstein, *Gates of Eden.*

2. Jerry Falwell, *The Fundamentalist Phenomenon: The Resurgence of Conservative Christianity* (Garden City, N.Y.: Doubleday, 1981), p. 190.

3. Jerry Falwell, *Listen America!* (Garden City, N.Y.: Doubleday, 1980), p. 20.

4. Falwell, *The Fundamentalist Phenomenon*, p. 213.

5. Ibid.

6. Falwell, *Listen America!*, p. 16.

7. Ibid., p. 18..

8. Ibid.

9. Ibid., p. 19.

10. Ibid., p. 20.

11. Ibid., p. 22-23.

12. Ibid., p. 95.

13. Ibid., p. 5.

14. Ibid., p. 20.

15. Ibid., p. 84-85.

16. Ibid., p. 85.

17. Ibid., p. 243.

18. Ibid., p. 244.

19. Frances FitzGerald, "A Reporter At Large: A Disciplined Charging Army," *The New Yorker*, May 18, 1981, p. 106.

20. FitzGerald, pp. 107-108.

21. Tim LaHaye, *The Battle for the Mind* (Old Tappan, N.J.: Fleming H. Revell Company, 1980), pp. 137-38.

22. William H. Marshner, "The New Creatures and the New Politics" (Washington: Committee for the Survival of a Free Congress, 1981), p. 24.

23. Francis A. Schaeffer, *A Christian Manifesto* (Westchester, Ill.: Crossway Books, 1981), p. 115.

24. Arthur Schlesinger, Jr., quoted in *America After Vietnam: A Series of Conversations Hosted by Daniel Schorr* (St. Paul: Twin Cities Public Television, 1979), p. 33.

Chapter 8

1.   Morton M. Kondracke, "Talking Ourselves into Breaking Up the Alliance?" *Wall Street Journal,* January 7, 1982, p. 19.
2.   Acheson, *Present at the Creation,* p. 726.
3.   Richard Nixon, *The Real War* (New York: Warner Books, 1981), p. 4.
4.   Cf. John F. Kennedy, *The Strategy of Peace,* ed. Allan Nevins (New York: Harper and Row, 1960), especially p. 62.
5.   Stanley Hoffmann, in Pfeffer, ed., *No More Vietnams?,* p. 116.
6.   R. W. B. Lewis, *The American Adam: Innocence, Tragedy, and Tradition in the Nineteenth Century* (Chicago: University of Chicago Press, 1955).
7.   Ibid., p. 198.
8.   *Wall Street Journal,* February 4, 1981, p. 3.
9.   Bernard Gwertzman, "President Sharply Assails Kremlin," *New York Times,* January 30, 1981, p. A1.
10.   Ruby Abramson, "Reagan Honors a Hero, Thanks Vietnam-Era Veterans," *Los Angeles Times,* February 25, 1981, part I, p. 9.
11.   Hedrick Smith, "Reagan's World," in Hedrick Smith et al., *Reagan: The Man, The President* (New York: Macmillan, 1980), p. 99.
12.   Nixon, *The Real War,* p. xv.
13.   Rowland Evans and Robert Novak, *The Reagan Revolution* (New York: E. P. Dutton, 1981), p. 208.
14.   Compare the heroes cited in Ronald Reagan's "What July Fourth Means to Me," *Parade,* June 28, 1981, p. 5, with those cited by Jerry Falwell in the chapter "Freedom's Heritage," in *Listen America!,* especially pp. 40-41.
15.   Bernard Weinraub, "U.S. Veterans End Trip to Vietnam," *New York Times,* December 25, 1981, p. A1.

Bibliography

Abrams, Floyd. "The Pentagon Papers a Decade Later." *The New York Times Magazine*, July 26, 1981, 22.

Acheson ,Dean. *Present at the Creation: My Years in the State Department*. New York: Norton, 1969.

Ambrose, Stephen E., and Barber, James A., Jr., eds. *The Military and American Society*. New York: Free Press, 1972.

Armstrong, Ben. *The Electric Church*. New York: Thomas Nelson, 1979.

Arnett, Peter, and MacLear, Michael. *Vietnam: The Ten Thousand Day War*. Garden City: Doubleday, 1981.

Austin, Anthony. *The President's War*. Philadelphia: Lippincott, 1971.

Baker, Mark. *Nam*. New York: Morrow, 1981.

Ball, George W. "Top Secret: The Prophecy the President Rejected." *The Atlantic*, July 1972, 36–49.

Baral, Jaya K. *The Pentagon and the Making of Foreign Policy: A Case Study of Vietnam: 1960-1968*. Atlantic Highlands, New Jersey: Humanities Press, 1978.

Baskir, Lawrence M., and Strauss, William A. *Chance and Circumstance: The Draft, the War and the Vietnam Generation*. New York: Knopf, 1978.

– – –. *Reconciliation After Vietnam*. South Bend, Ind.: University of Notre Dame Press, 1977.

Bell, D. Bruce, and Houston, Thomas J. *The Vietnam Era Deserter: Characteristics of Unconvicted Army Deserters Participating in the Presidential Clemency Program*. U.S. Army Research Institute for the Behavioral and Social Sciences, July 1976.

Bergman, Arlene Eisen. *Women of Vietnam*. San Francisco: People's Press, 1974.

Berrigan, Daniel. *Night Flight to Hanoi: War Diary with 11 Poems*. New York: Macmillan, 1968.

Blakey, Scott. *Prisoner at War: The Survival of Commander Richard A. Stratton.* Garden City: Doubleday, 1978.

Bleir, Rocky, and O'Neil, Terry. *Fighting Back.* Briarcliff Manor, New York: Stein & Day, 1980.

Bodard, Lucien. *The Quicksand War: Prelude to Vietnam.* Translated by Patrick O'Brian. Boston: Little, Brown, 1967.

Bonds, Ray, ed. *The Vietnam War: The Illustrated History of the Conflict in Southeast Asia.* New York: Crown, 1979.

Bouscaren, Anthony T. *The Last of the Mandarins: Diem of Vietnam.* Pittsburgh: Duquesne University Press, 1965.

Boyle, Richard. *Flower of the Dragon: The Breakdown of the U.S. Army in Vietnam.* Palo Alto: Ramparts, 1972.

Braestrup, Peter. *Big Story: How the American Press and Television Reported and Interpreted the Crisis of Tet 1968 in Vietnam and Washington.* 2 vols. Boulder: Westview Press, 1977.

Brandon, Harry. *Anatomy of Error.* Boston: Gambit, 1969.

Brinton, Crane. *The Anatomy of Revolution.* New York: Random House, 1938.

Browne, Malcolm W. *The New Face of War.* Indianapolis: Bobbs-Merrill, 1965.

Bryan, C. D. B. *Friendly Fire.* New York: Putnam, 1976.

Bundy, McGeorge. "Vietnam, Watergate and Presidential Powers." *Foreign Affairs* 58, no. 2, Winter 1979–1980, 397-407.

Burns, Richard D., and Leitenberg, Milton. *A Guide to the Vietnam Conflict.* Santa Barbara: ABC Clio, 1982.

Buttinger, Joseph. *A Dragon Embattled.* 2 vols. New York: Praeger, 1967.

– – –. *The Smaller Dragon: A Political History of Vietnam.* New York: Praeger, 1958.

Cao-Ky, Nguyen. *Twenty Years and Twenty Days.* Briarcliff Manor, New York: Stein & Day, 1976.

Capps, Walter H. "The Vietnam Experience: A World of Broken Pieces." *The Center Magazine*, September-October 1979, 49.

– – –. "The War's Transformation." *The Center Magazine*, July-August, 1978, 18.

Caputo, Philip. *A Rumor of War.* New York: Holt, Rinehart & Winston, 1977.

– – –. "The Unreturning Army." *Playboy*. Vol. 29, January 1982, 106.

Carver, George. "The Real Revolution in South Vietnam." *Foreign Affairs* 43, April 1965, 387–408.

Chandler, Robert W. *War of Ideas: The U.S. Propaganda Campaign in Vietnam*. Boulder: Westview, 1981.

Charlton, Michael, and Moncrieff, Anthony. *Many Reasons Why: The American Involvement in Vietnam*. New York: Hill & Wang, 1978.

Chomsky, Noam. *American Power and the New Mandarins*. New York: Random House, 1967.

– – –. *At War With Asia*. New York: Random House, 1970.

– – –. *For Reasons of State*. New York: Random House, 1973.

– – –. *Towards a New Cold War: Essays on the Current Crisis and How We Got There*. New York: Pantheon, 1982.

Clifford, Clark M. "A Viet Nam Reappraisal." *Foreign Affairs* 47, no. 4, July 1969, 601-622.

Condominas, Georges. *We Have Eaten the Forest: The Story of a Montagnard Village in the Central Highlands of Vietnam*. New York: Hill & Wang, 1977.

Connecticut Mutual Life Report on American Values in the '80s: The Impact of Belief, The. Research and Forecasts, Inc., 1980.

Cooper, Chester L. *The Lost Crusade*. New York: Dodd, Mead, 1970.

Corder, E. M. *The Deer Hunter*. New York: E.M.I. Films, 1978.

Corson, William R. *The Betrayal*. New York: Norton, 1968.

– – –. *The Consequences of Failure*. New York: Norton, 1974.

Cortright, David. *Soldiers in Revolt: The American Military Today*. Garden City: Doubleday, 1975.

Cox, Harvey. *Turning East: The Promise and Peril of the New Orientalism*. New York: Simon & Schuster, 1977.

Crawford, Alan. *Thunder on the Right: The "New Right" and the Politics of Resentment*. New York: Pantheon, 1980.

Critchfield, Richard. *The Long Charade: Political Subversion in the Vietnam War*. New York: Harcourt Brace Jovanovich, 1968.

Dallek, Robert. *Franklin D. Roosevelt and American Foreign Policy, 1932–1945*. New York: Oxford University Press, 1979.

Dawson, Alan. *55 Days: The Fall of South Vietnam*. Englewood Cliffs: Prentice-Hall, 1977.

Deitchman, Seymour J. *The Best-Laid Schemes: A Tale of Social Research and Bureaucracy*. Cambridge: Massachusetts Institute of Technology Press, 1976.

Dickstein, Morris. *Gates of Eden: American Culture in the Sixties*. New York: Basic Books, 1977.

Downs, Frederick. *The Killing Zone: My Life in the Vietnam War*. New York: Norton, 1978.

Dramesi, John A. *A Code of Honor*. New York: Norton, 1975.

Drinan, Robert F. *Vietnam and Armageddon: Peace, War and the Christian Conscience*. New York : Sheed and Ward, 1970.

Duffett, John, ed. *Against the Crime of Silence: Proceedings of the Russell International War Crimes Tribunal, 1967*. New York: Simon & Schuster, 1970.

Duncanson, Dennis J. *Government and Revolution in Vietnam*. New York: Oxford University Press, 1968.

Dung, Van Tien. *Our Great Spring Victory: An Account of the Liberation of South Vietnam*. Translated by John Speagens. New York: Monthly Review Press, 1977.

Earley, Pete. "Forgotten Women: Effects of War on Female Vietnam Veterans Are Only Now Emerging." *The Washington Post*, March 25, 1981, A1, A13.

Eisenhower, Dwight D. *Mandate for Change, 1953–1956*. Garden City: Doubleday, 1963.

Ellsberg, Daniel. *Papers on the War*. New York: Simon & Schuster, 1972.

Emerson, Gloria. *Winners and Loser: Battles, Retreats, Gains, Losses, and Ruins from a Long War*. New York: Random House, 1977.

Evans, Rowland, and Novak, Robert. *The Reagan Revolution*. New York: Dutton, 1981.

Falk, Richard A. *The Vietnam War and International Law*. 4 vols. Princeton: Princeton University Press, 1976.

Fall, Bernard B. *Last Reflections on a War*. Garden City: Doubleday, 1967.

– – –. *"The Political-Religious Sects of Viet-Nam."* Public Affairs 28, September 1955, 235–253.

– – –. *Street Without Joy: Insurgency in Indochina, 1946–1963*. Harrisburg: Stackpole, 1963.

– – –. *The Two Vietnams: A Political and Military Analysis*. New York: Praeger, 1963.

– – –. *Vietnam Witness, 1953–1966.* New York: Praeger, 1966.

Falwell, Jerry, ed. *The Fundamentalist Phenomenon: The Resurgence of Conservative Christianity.* Garden City: Doubleday, 1982.

– – –. *Listen, America!.* Garden City: Doubleday, 1980.

Fanning, Louis A. *Betrayal In Vietnam.* New Rochelle: Arlington House, 1976.

Fenn, Charles. *Ho Chi Minh: A Biographical Introduction.* New York: Scribner, 1973.

Ferber, Michael, and Lynd, Staughton. *The Resistance.* Boston: Beacon Press, 1971.

Figley, Charles R., ed. *Stress Disorders Among Vietnam Veterans: Theory, Research and Treatment Implications.* New York: Brunner/Mazel, 1978.

Finn, James. *Conscience and Command.* New York: Random House, 1971.

Fishel, Wesley R., ed. *Vietnam: Anatomy of a Conflict.* Itasca, Ill.: F. E. Peacock, 1968.

FitzGerald, Frances. "A Disciplined Charging Army." *The New Yorker,* May 18, 1981, 53.

– – –. *Fire in the Lake: The Vietnamese and the Americans in Vietnam.* Boston: Little, Brown, 1972.

Flood, Charles Bracelen. *The War of the Innocents.* New York: McGraw-Hill, 1970.

Ford, Gerald R. *A Time to Heal.* New York: Harper & Row, 1979.

Fussell, Paul. *The Great War and Modern Memory.* New York: Oxford University Press, 1975.

Gallucci, Robert L. *Neither Peace Nor Honor: The Politics of American Military Policy in Viet-Nam.* Baltimore: Johns Hopkins University Press, 1975.

Gallup, George, Jr., and Poling, David. *The Search for America's Faith.* Nashville: Abingdon, 1980.

Gardner, John. *Morale.* New York: Norton, 1978.

Gelb, Leslie. "The Essential Domino: American Politics and Vietnam." *Foreign Affairs,* April 1972, 459–475.

– – –. "Vietnam: The System Worked." *Foreign Policy* 3, Summer 1971, 140-167.

Gelb, Leslie, and Betts, Richard K. *The Irony of Vietnam.* Washington: Brookings Institution, 1979.

Geyelin, Philip. *Lyndon Johnson and the World.* New York: Praeger, 1966.

Glasser, Ronald J. *Three Hundred Sixty-Five Days.* New York: George Braziller, 1971.

Goodman, Allen E. *The Lost Peace: America's Search for a Negotiated Settlement of the Vietnam War.* Stanford: Hoover Institute Press, 1978.

– – –. *Politics in War: The Bases of Political Community in South Vietnam.* Stanford: Hoover Institute Press, 1978.

Gough, Kathleen. *Ten Times More Beautiful: The Rebuilding of Vietnam.* New York: Monthly Review Press, 1978.

Goulden, Joseph C. *Truth Is the First Casualty: The Gulf of Tonkin Affair – Illusion and Reality.* Chicago: Rand McNally, 1969.

Graff, Henry. *The Tuesday Cabinet.* Englewood Cliffs: Prentice-Hall, 1970.

Griffen, William L., and Marciano, John. *Teaching the Vietnam War.* Montclair, N.H.: Allanheld Osmun, 1979.

Halberstam, David. *The Best and the Brightest.* Greenwich: Fawcett, 1969.

– – –. *The Making of a Quagmire.* New York: Random House, 1965.

– – –. "Return to Vietnam." *Harper's,* December 1967, 47–58.

– – –. "Voices of the Vietcong." *Harper's,* January 1968, 45–52.

Halstead, Fred. *GI's Speak Out Against the War.* New York: Pathfinder, 1970.

– – –. *Out Now! A Participant's Account of the American Movement Against the Vietnam War.* New York: Monad Press, 1978.

Hammer, Ellen J. *Vietnam Yesterday and Today.* New York: Holt, Rinehart & Winston, 1966.

Hauser, William L. *America's Army in Crisis.* Baltimore: Johns Hopkins University Press, 1973.

Heath, G. Louis. *Meeting Does Not Happen Lightly: The Literature of the American Resistance to the Vietnam War.* Metuchen, New Jersey: Scarecrow Press, 1976.

Helmer, John. *Bringing the War Home: The American Soldier in Vietnam and After.* New York: Free Press, 1974.

Herr, Michael. *Dispatches.* New York: Knopf, 1977.

Herring, George C. *America's Longest War: The U.S. and Vietnam 1950 to 1975.* New York: John Wiley, 1979.

Hersh, Seymour. *My Lai 4.* New York: Random House, 1970.

Hickey, Gerald C. *Village in Vietnam.* New Haven: Yale University Press, 1964.

Hilsman, Roger. *To Move a Nation: The Politics of Foreign Policy in the Administration of John F. Kennedy.* Garden City: Doubleday, 1967.

Honey, P. J. *Genesis of a Tragedy: The Historical Background to the Vietnam War.* London: Benn, 1968.

Horne, A. D., ed. *The Wounded Generation: America After Vietnam.* Englewood Cliffs: Prentice-Hall, 1981.

Hosmer, Stephen T.; Kellen, Konrad; and Jenkins, Brian M. *The Fall of South Vietnam: Statements by Vietnamese Military and Civilian Leaders.* Santa Monica: The Rand Corporation, December 1978.

Hubbell, John G., et al. *P.O.W. A Definitive History of the American Prisoner-of-War Experience in Vietnam.* New York: Reader's Digest Press, 1976.

Janowitz, Morris. *The New Military.* New York: Russell Sage Foundation, 1971.

Johnson, Lyndon Baines. *The Vantage Point: Perspectives of the Presidency 1963-1969.* New York: Holt, Rinehart & Winston, 1971.

Joiner, Charles A. *The Politics of Massacre: Political Processes in South Vietnam.* Philadelphia: Temple University Press, 1974.

Just, Ward. *To What End.* Boston: Houghton Mifflin, 1968.

Kagan, Robert W. "Realities and Myths of the Vietnam War." *The Wall Street Journal,* April 1, 1982, 1.

Kail, F. M. *What Washington Said: Administration Rhetoric and the Vietnam War, 1949-1969.* New York: Harper & Row, 1973.

Kalb, Marvin, and Abel, Elie. *Roots of Involvement: The U.S. in Asia 1784-1971.* New York: Norton, 1971.

Kalb, Marvin, and Kalb, Bernard. *Kissinger.* Boston: Little, Brown, 1974.

Kendrick, Alexander. *The World Within: America in the Vietnam Years, 1945-1974.* Boston: Little, Brown, 1974.

Kennedy, John F. *The Strategy of Peace.* Edited by Allan Nevins. New York: Harper & Row, 1960.

Kennedy, Robert F. *To Seek a Newer World.* New York: Bantam, 1968.

King, Martin Luther. "Declaration of Independence from the War in Vietnam." *Ramparts* V, no. 11, May 1967, 33.

Kissinger, Henry. "The Viet Nam Negotiations." *Foreign Affairs* 47, no. 2, January 1969, 211-234.

– – –. *White House Years.* Boston: Little, Brown, 1979.

– – –. *Years of Upheaval.* Boston: Little, Brown, 1982.

Klinkowitz, Jerome, and Somer, John, eds. *Writing Under Fire: Stories of the Vietnam War.* New York: Dell, 1978.

Kovic, Ron. *Born on the Fourth of July.* New York: McGraw-Hill, 1976.

Kurland, Gerald, ed. *The United States in Vietnam.* New York: Simon & Schuster, 1975.

Lacouture, Jean. *Ho Chi Minh: A Political Biography.* Translated by Peter Wiles. New York: Random House, 1968.

– – –. *Vietnam: Between Two Truces.* Translated by Konrad Kellen and Joel Carmichael. New York: Random House, 1966.

Lake, Anthony, ed. *The Legacy of Vietnam. The War, American Society, and the Future of American Foreign Policy.* New York: New York University Press, 1976.

Lang, Daniel. *Patriotism Without Flags* New York: Norton, 1974.

Lasch, Christopher. *The Culture of Narcissism: American Life in An Age of Diminishing Expectations.* New York: Norton, 1978.

Lawson, Don. *The War in Vietnam.* New York: Franklin Watts, 1981.

Leckie, Robert. *The Wars of America: A Comprehensive Narrative. From Champlain's First Campaign Against the Iroquois Through the End of the Vietnam War.* New York: Harper & Row, 1981.

Lederer, William J. *Our Own Worst Enemy.* New York: Norton, 1968.

Lewis, R. W. B. *The American Adam: Innocence, Tragedy, and Tradition in the Nineteenth Century.* Chicago: University of Chicago Press, 1955.

Lewy, Guenter. *America in Vietnam.* New York: Oxford University Press, 1978.

Lifton, Robert Jay. *Home from the War: Vietnam Veterans: Neither Victims nor Executioners.* New York: Simon & Schuster, 1973.

Limqueco, Peter, and Weiss, Peter, eds. *International War Crimes Tribunal–Prevent the Crime of Silence.* London: Allen Lane, 1971.

Linenthal, Edward Tabor. "The Warrior as a Symbolic Figure in America" Ph.D. dissertation, University of California, 1979.

Liska, George. *War and Order: Reflections on Vietnam and History.* Baltimore: Johns Hopkins University Press, 1968.

Loory, Stuary H. *Defeated: Inside America's Military Machine.* New York: Random House, 1973.

Luce, Don, and Sommer, John. *Vietnam: The Unheard Voices.* Ithaca: Cornell University Press, 1969.

Lynd, Alice. *We Won't Go.* Boston: Beacon Press, 1968.

Magee, Doug. "The Long War of Wayne Felde." *The Nation,* January 2–9, 1982, 11–14.

Manning, Robert, and Janeway, Michael. *Who We Are: An Atlantic Chronicle of the United States and Vietnam 1966–1969.* Boston: Little, Brown, 1969.

Marin, Peter. "Coming to Terms with Vietnam." *Harper's,* December 1980, 41–56.

– – –. "Living in Mortal Pain." *Psychology Today* 15, November 1981, 68.

McAlister, John T. *Vietnam: The Origins of Revolution.* New York: Knopf, 1969.

– – –, and Mus, Paul. *The Vietnamese and Their Revolution.* New York: Harper & Row, 1970.

McCarthy, Mary. *Hanoi.* New York: Harcourt Brace Jovanovich, 1968.

– – –. *Medina.* New York: Harcourt Brace Jovanovich, 1972.

– – –. *The Seventeenth Degree.* New York: Harcourt Brace Jovanovich, 1974.

McCubbin, Hamilton J. *Family Separation and Reunion.* San Diego: Center for Prisoner of War Studies, Naval Health Research Center, 1974.

McGarvey, Patrick J. *Visions of Victory: Selected Vietnamese Communist Military Writings, 1964–1968.* Stanford: Hoover Institute Press, 1969.

Mecklin, John. *Mission in Torment: An Intimate Account of the U.S. Role in Vietnam.* Garden City: Doubleday, 1965.

Millett, Allan R., ed. *A Short History of the Vietnam War.* Bloomington: Indiana University Press, 1978.

Milstein, Jeffrey S. *Dynamics of the Vietnam War.* Columbus: Ohio State University Press, 1974.

Minh, Ho Chi. *Selected Writings 1920–1969.* Hanoi: Foreign Languages Publishing House, 1973.

Moore, John N. *Law and the Indo-China War.* Princeton: Princeton University Press, 1972.

Morris, Ivan. *The Nobility of Failure.* New York: Holt, Rinehart & Winston, 1975.

Mullen, Robert M. *Blacks in America's Wars: The Shift in Attitudes from the Revolutionary War to Vietnam.* New York: Monad Press, 1973.

Murphy, Rae. *Vietnam: Impressions of a People's War.* Toronto: Canadian Tribune, 1967.

Mus, Paul. "Viet Nam: A Nation Off Balance." *Yale Review* 41, Summer 1952, 524-538.

Neumann-Hoditz, Reinhold. *Portrait of Ho Chi Minh: An Illustrated Biography.* Translated by John Hargreaves. New York: Herder and Herder, 1972.

Nixon, Richard. *The Real War.* New York: Warner Books, 1980.

– – –. *RN: The Memoirs of Richard Nixon.* New York: Grosset & Dunlap, 1978.

Oberdorfer, Don. *Tet!.* Garden City: Doubleday, 1971.

O'Brien, Tim. *If I Die in a Combat Zone, Box Me Up and Ship Me Home.* New York: Dell, 1969.

– – –. *Going After Cacciato.* New York: Delacorte, 1975.

Parker, Maynard. "Vietnam: The War That Won't End." *Foreign Affairs* 53, January 1975, 352–374.

Patti, Archimedes L. *Why Vietnam: Prelude to America's Albatross.* Berkeley: University of California Press, 1981.

Peace in Vietnam: A New Approach in Southeast Asia (A Report Prepared for the American Friends Service Committee). New York: Hill & Wang, 1966.

The Pentagon Papers, as published by *The New York Times,* written by Neil Sheehan, Hedrick Smith, E. W. Kenworthy, and Fox Butterfield. New York: Bantam, 1971.

– – –. U.S. Department of Defense (The Senator Gravel edition). Boston: Beacon Press, 1971.

Peterson, Iver. "Vietnam Veterans Parade in Shadow of 52 Hostages." *The New York Times,* February 1, 1981, 22.

Pfeffer, Richard M., ed. *No More Vietnams? The War and the Future of American Foreign Policy.* New York: Harper & Row, 1968.

Pike, Douglas. *Viet Cong.* Cambridge: Massachusetts Institute of Technology Press, 1966.

– – –. *War, Peace, and the Viet Cong.* Boston: Massachusetts Institute of Technology Press, 1969.

Podhoretz, Norman. "A Note of Vietnamization." *Commentary,* May 1971, 9.

– – –. *Why We Were in Vietnam*. New York: Simon & Schuster, 1982.

Polner, Murray. *No Victory Parades: The Return of the Vietnam Veteran*. New York: Holt, Rinehart & Winston, 1971.

Porter, Garth. *A Peace Denied: The United States, Vietnam and the Paris Agreement*. Bloomington: Indiana University Press, 1976.

– – –. ed. *Vietnam: A History in Documents*. New York: New American Library, 1981.

Powers, Thomas. *The War at Home*. New York: Grossman, 1973.

Race, Jeffrey. *War Comes to Long An*. Berkeley: University of California Press, 1972.

Radvanyi, Janos. *Delusion and Reality: Gambits, Hoaxes and Diplomatic One-Upmanship in Vietnam*. Chicago: Regnery/Gateway, 1978.

Randall, Margaret. *Spirit of the People*. Vancouver: New Star Books, 1975.

Reischauer, Edwin O. *Beyond Vietnam: The United States and Asia*. New York: Random House, 1967.

Roberts, Chalmers M. "Foreign Policy Under a Paralyzed Presidency," *Foreign Affairs* 52, no. 4, July 1974, 675.

Rostow, Walt W. *The Diffusion of Power*. New York: Macmillan, 1972.

Rowan, Stephen A. *They Wouldn't Let Us Die: The Prisoners of War Tell Their Story*. New York: Jonathan David, 1975.

Russell, Bertrand. *War Crimes in Vietnam*. New York: Monthly Review, 1967.

Santoli, Al. *Everything We Had. An Oral History of the Vietnam War by Thirty-Three American Soldiers Who Fought It*. New York: Random House, 1981.

Schandler, Herbert Y. *The Unmaking of a President: Lyndon Johnson and Vietnam*. Princeton: Princeton University Press, 1977.

Scheer, Robert. *How the United States Got Involved in Vietnam*. Santa Barbara: Center for the Study of Democratic Institutions, 1965.

Schell, Jonathan. *The Military Half*. New York: Knopf, 1968.

– – –. *The Village of Ben Suc*. New York: Knopf, 1967.

Schemmer, Benjamin F. *The Raid*. New York: Harper & Row, 1976.

Schevitz, Jeffrey. *The Weaponsmakers: Personal and Professional Crisis During the Vietnam War*. Cambridge: Schenkman, 1979.

Schlesinger, Arthur M., Jr. *The Bitter Heritage: Vietnam and American Democracy, 1941–1966*. Boston: Houghton Mifflin, 1967.

– – –. *Robert Kennedy and His Times*. 2 vols. Boston: Houghton Mifflin, 1978.

Schoenbrun, David. *Vietnam: How We Got In. How to Get Out*. New York: Atheneum, 1968.

Schorr, Daniel (host). *America After Vietnam: A Series of Conversations*. St. Paul: Twin Cities Public Television, 1979.

Scigliano, Robert G. *South Vietnam: Nation Under Stress*. Boston: Houghton Mifflin, 1964.

Sennett, Richard. *The Fall of Public Man: On the Social Psychology of Capitalism*. New York: Random House, 1978.

Shaplen, Robert. *The Lost Revolution: The U.S. in Vietnam, 1946–1966*. New York: Harper & Row, 1966.

– – –. *The Road from War: Vietnam, 1965–1970*. New York: Harper & Row, 1971.

Shawcross, William. *Side-Show: Kissinger, Nixon and the Destruction of Cambodia*. New York: Simon & Schuster, 1979.

Sherrill, Robert. *Military Justice Is to Justice as Military Music Is to Music*. New York: Harper & Row, 1970.

Shibata, Shingo. *Lessons of the Vietnam War: Philosophical Considerations on the Vietnam Revolution*. Atlantic Highlands, N.J.: Humanities Press, 1973.

Simon, William E. *A Time for Truth*. New York: Reader's Digest Press, 1978.

Smith, Hedrick; Clymer, Adam; Silk, Leonard; Lindsey, Robert; and Burt, Richard. *Reagan the Man, the President*. New York: Macmillan, 1980.

Sochurek, Howard. "Americans in Action in Viet Nam." *National Geographic*, January 1965, 38–65.

Sontag, Susan. *Trip to Hanoi*. New York: Farrar, Straus & Giroux, 1968.

Starr, Paul, et al. *The Discarded Army: Veterans After Vietnam*. New York: Charterhouse, 1974.

Starry, Donn A. *Armored Combat in Vietnam*. Indianapolis: Bobbs-Merrill, 1981.

Stavina, Ralph; Barnet, Richard J.; and Raskin, Marcus G. *Washington Plans an Aggressive War*. New York: Random House, 1971.

Summers, Harry G., Jr. "U. S. Army Strategy in Vietnam: A Critique." *The Wall Street Journal*, April 21, 1982, 28.

Szulc, Tad. *The Illusion of Peace*. New York: Viking, 1978.

Tauber, Peter. *The Last Best Hope.* New York: Harcourt Brace Jovanovich, 1977.

– – –. *The Sunshine Soldiers.* New York: Simon & Schuster, 1971.

Taylor, Maxwell. *Swords and Plowshares.* New York: Norton, 1972.

Taylor. Telford. *Nurenberg and Vietnam: An American Tragedy.* New
York: Bantam, 1971.

Terkel, Studs. *American Dreams: Lost and Found.* New York:
Pantheon, 1980.

Terzani, Tiziano. *Giai Phong: The Fall and Liberation of Saigon.* New
York: St. Martin's Press, 1976.

Thies, Wallace J. *When Governments Collide: Coercion and Diplomacy
in the Vietnam Conflict, 1964–1968.* Berkeley: University of California Press, 1980.

Thompson, Robert. *No Exit From Vietnam.* New York: McKay, 1969.

Thompson, W. Scott, and Frizzell, Donaldson D., eds. *The Lessons of
Vietnam.* New York: Crane, Russak, 1977.

Trooboff, Peter D., ed. *Law and Responsibility in Warfare: The Vietnam
Experience.* Chapel Hill: University of North Carolina Press, 1975.

Tsongas, Paul. *The Road From Here: Liberalism and Realities in the
1980s.* New York: Knopf, 1981.

Turner, Kathleen. *The Press and Johnson's Vietnam Rhetoric.* Ames,
Iowa: Iowa State University Press, 1980.

Turner, Robert F. *Vietnamese Communism: Its Origins and Development.* Stanford: Hoover Institute Press, 1975.

Uhl, Michael, and Ensign, Tod. *G.I. Guinea Pigs: How the Pentagon
Exposed Our Troops to Dangers More Deadly Than War.* New York:
Harper & Row, 1980.

Useem, Michael. *Conscription, Protest and Social Conflict: The Life and
Death of a Draft Resistance Movement.* New York: John Wiley, 1973.

Viorst, Milton. *Fire in the Streets.* New York: Simon & Schuster, 1979.

Walters, Vernon A. *Silent Missions.* Garden City: Doubleday, 1978.

Walzer, Michael. *Radical Principles. Reflections of an Unreconstructed
Democrat.* New York: Basic Books, 1980.

– – –. "Were We Wrong About Vietnam?" *New Republic* 181, August
18, 1979, 15.

Warner, Denis. *Certain Victory: How Hanoi Won the War.* Kansas City:
Sheed Andrews and McMeel, 1977.

Waterhouse, Carry G., and Wizard, Marianna G. *Turning the Guns
Around: Notes on the G.I. Movement.* New York: Praeger, 1971.

Webb, Kate. *On the Other Side. Twenty-Three Days with the Viet Cong.* New York: New York Times Books, 1972.

West, F. J. *The Village.* New York: Harper & Row, 1972.

Westmoreland, William C. *Report on the War in Vietnam.* Washington: Government Printing Office, 1969.

– – –. *A Soldier Reports.* Garden City: Doubleday, 1976.

Windchy, Eugene G. *Tonkin Gulf.* Garden City: Doubleday, 1971.

Wofford, Harris. *Of Kennedys and Kings: Making Sense of the Sixties.* New York: Farrar, Straus & Giroux, 1980.

Woodside, Alexander B. *Community and Revolution in Modern Vietnam.* Boston: Houghton Mifflin, 1976.

Woodstone, Norma Sue. *Up Against the War.* New York: Tower, 1970.

Woodward, Bob, and Bernstein, Carl. *The Final Days.* New York: Simon & Schuster, 1976.

Index

Walter Capps, former director of the Robert Hutchins Center for the Study of Democratic Institutions, is professor of religious studies at the University of California, Santa Barbara. He has written and edited eight books, including *Silent Fire: An Invitation to Western Mysticism* and *Seeing with the Native Eye: Essays on Native American Religion.*